Transforming Toxic Leaders

Transforming Toxic Leaders

Alan Goldman

Stanford Business Books

An Imprint of Stanford University Press

Stanford, California 2009

Stanford University Press
Stanford, California

Library of Congress Cataloging-in-Publication Data

Goldman, Alan
    Transforming toxic leaders / Alan Goldman
        p. cm.
    Includes bibliographical references and index.
    ISBN 978-0-8047-5828-4 (cloth : alk. paper)

    1. Leadership.   2. Executives—Psychology.   3. Executive ability.   4. Management.
I. Title.

    HD57.7.G6639   2006
    658.4'092—dc22   2009007955

Typeset at Stanford University Press in 10/14 Minion

Special discounts for bulk quantities of Stanford Business Books are available to corporations,
professional associations, and other organizations. For details and discount information,
contact the special sales department of Stanford University Press. Tel: (650) 736-1783, Fax:
(650) 736-1784

CONTENTS

EXTENDED TABLE OF CONTENTS

Acknowledgments

The Visible and the Invisible

Writing a book is a journey. Traveling through new terrain, making sense of the wilds, and persevering through the highs and lows requires close relationships and camaraderie. I begin by acknowledging my most prominent and visible influences and at the conclusion make reference to the sometimes invisible forces shaping the passion and commitment culminating in a major endeavor.

First and foremost I acknowledge my extraordinary colleague David Van Fleet. I cannot count how many times I showed up in David's office or stopped him in the hallway to get his views and reactions to my ideas. David Van Fleet is a one-of-a-kind colleague. His keen insights, detailed knowledge of the management field, and sobriety kept me on track. Also, I must make mention of another special colleague down the hallway, Fred Walumbwa. Fred was particularly present during the early days of this project when ideas were germinating. While Fred's son, John Henry, ran the hallways with my son, Ben, there were fertile discussions and creations born of my talks with Fred. Also, the belief and support of my former dean, Gary Waissi, was a strong and positive factor—he had complete faith in me and in this project. I must also acknowledge my Academy of Management colleague David Jamieson, who serves as an editor for the *Journal of Management Inquiry*. My recent publication for JMI on toxicity in leaders and organizations was guided by David. Also, there is much reason to acknowledge a superior former member of our administrative staff, Joan Jankowski. Joan not only worked with the manuscript from beginning to end; she also was instrumental in bringing form to my ideas via her creation and layouts of Figures 1 and 2—key blueprints for the book. Many thanks to Joan

Jankowski! Also, I would like to thank my special friend and colleague Professor Jane Carey, who helped me with a revision of the second figure and read the minds of my editors and myself in a matter of minutes.

My acknowledgments would be incomplete without calling attention to the pivotal role of Dr. Geoffrey Burn, Director of Stanford University Press. Geoffrey was enthusiastic and supportive throughout this project. At the Academy of Management Conference in Philadelphia we had a chance to sit down and talk about the book face-to-face. I instantly knew that I was very fortunate to be building a relationship with both Geoffrey Burn and Stanford University Press. It's not often that one makes precisely the right connection. Without Geoffrey's belief in me this project as it has developed would not exist. For this I am extremely grateful.

On a personal note, my son, Ben, and my daughter, Olivia, provided a special kind of support throughout the writing of the book. Frequently I spoke out loud and bounced ideas off of my kids to get their reactions. Their bright and insightful responses often influenced my thinking and brought me closer to clarity. And a special acknowledgment and thank you goes out to my dear mother, Shirley. For hours at a time we have discussed everything under the sun, including the stories and ideas that populate this book. Her lifelong career in business and real estate provided Mom with uncanny insights into the nature of people and the whole of human behavior. Suffice it to say, Mom is always involved, and she was a core influence on the guy who wrote this book. I must also acknowledge my soccer-playing, fisherman, and businessman dad, Sol Goldman. I am very thankful to my dad for training and coaching me through my competition in table tennis and my New York City tournament victory. But most of all, Dad taught me that life was an adventure through our early fishing trips in upstate New York. He showed me that I have the power to make my own good times. Although Dad departed before I began this book, my years with him and his drive to get to the bottom of things deeply influenced me. And I must also mention my sensitive sister Ruth, who has always been supportive and insightful.

Other strong influences include my amazing sister Susan and her husband, Stanley—who as brilliant and renowned attorneys provided a perspective somewhat alien and apart from that of social science researchers and academicians. My personal involvement in trial law has awakened my understanding of the rigor and precision of their assessments and decision-making on the firing line. Our discussions about human behavior, motives, hidden agendas, complex personalities, and brilliant but deviant professionals all deeply shaped my thinking. Toxicity and dysfunctional behavior are commonplace in civil, criminal, and corporate law.

In addition, I would be missing a rather large influence if I did not call attention to my Academy of Management brethren. Particularly within the ranks of the Management Consulting Division I have had the great fortune to associate with first-class scholars, coaches, and consultants who share their insider perspectives. I might also add that by virtue of winning two "top paper" awards in the Management Consulting Division over the past few years I came to increasingly trust my instincts and ability to synthesize and create bridges between management and organizational behavior scholarship and corporate consulting.

I particularly want to call attention to the leaders and organizations that are the main characters and entities in these pages. In serving as a leadership coach, management consultant, and organizational therapist I have been privileged to have access to information usually contained behind closed doors. The trials and tribulations of my clients have constituted the groundwork for my work on transformational change and the movement from toxicity and deficits to abundance and superior performance.

Finally, I would like to make brief note of the invisible and subconscious terrain that motivates me to want to climb the mountain, be on the frontiers of coaching, consulting, and research, and as the French Symbolist artists in the nineteenth century expressed it, "to search for the rose that is in no bouquet." In the course of writing this book I went through much self-assessment and many late-night diagnostics wondering why this subject matter intrigued me to the point of a serious focus and an obsessive commitment. Little by little I realized that the dark and occasionally toxic side of my personal relationships has been a trying and a fertile source of both deficits and abundance. The reservoir of disappointment, failure, and yearnings yields deep desire, turmoil, and a search for truth.

Trained as a social scientist and researcher as well as a counselor and therapist, I see both conscious and subconscious and visible and invisible dramas unfolding in leaders and organizations. I recognize the enigmatic and slippery terrain of human behavior. I have made every effort to maintain the complexity, nuance, and texture of my clients in these pages. Forgive me for altering their true names and reshaping the story lines, but it was absolutely necessary in order to maintain client confidentiality and to protect privileged communication. I have made every effort, however, not to compromise the thick narratives and complexity that are central to dysfunctional organizations and toxic leaders.

I am hopeful that as spokesperson and author I am able to do justice to my client organizations and leaders and to the many special people, entities, and forces mentioned above. I have made every effort to provide readers with an affective and thought-provoking book that provides direction in unraveling toxicity and moving toward personal and professional abundance.

Introduction

Differential Diagnosis: Coach, Consultant, and Client

> *The reckless behavior of a CEO can be studied and addressed*
> *at the level of the brain cell, the brain, the individual organism,*
> *the individual psyche, the executive team, the company and*
> *society. . . . A coach who is limited to one level only, and on that*
> *level to one method only, is like someone who uses a hammer to*
> *drive nails, fasten screws and bolts and even to paint. . . . From a*
> *systems point of view, however, this does not make any sense at all.*
> *Many very good hypotheses and explanations about issues such as*
> *leadership co-exist on different levels at the same time.*
> **—T. Compernolle, *Coach and Couch***

In this book I share a conversation that is taking place increasingly often behind closed corporate doors. It is a conversation frequently held between leadership coaches, management consultants, organizational scholars, and corporate clients. The line of questioning that tends to dominate these talks resonates in CEOs' chambers and trickles down to the factory floors of Fortune 500 firms. They are typically belated and reluctant inquiries into the darker, counterproductive, and destructive side of the workplace. The questions fall under the heading of toxic leadership:

- What do we do about leaders who are toxic? How do we handle high achievers who also bring deviant and destructive behaviors into our organizations?
- Why do colleagues, followers, and executive boards empower, shield, or avoid toxic leaders?
- Is there any way to positively address our concerns over the delicacy surrounding dealing with toxic leaders?
- How does an organization approach and request accountability from an absentee leader?

- Who in our organization is qualified and ready to assess and intervene when faced with destructive behavior? Can we act before the damage escalates?
- Why have our human resource experts, supervisors, and managers illustrated a lack of readiness or reluctance to respond to toxic behaviors?

When a CEO, a director of aerospace engineering, a business school dean, or a chief cardiac surgeon undermines productivity with condescending and demeaning behavior toward subordinates, how does this affect colleagues, customers, stakeholders, and the entire organization? Surely every corporate officer, president, and executive board member is entitled to a bad day, an occasional loss of temper, or a conflict with a subordinate. But what if the leader's behavior is part of an emotionally unintelligent pattern that negatively affects coworkers, wreaks havoc in the workplace, and spreads companywide? Does such behavior mean that he, or she, is a toxic leader?

THE STAKES ARE HIGH

The spread of destructive behavior requires scrutiny. As a toxic leader goes, so may the company go. Are toxic leaders individually grown and identifiable through DNA and brain mapping, or are they also the products of poisonous business environments? In the aftermath of more than a few corporate scandals (think Enron and Arthur Andersen), it has become fashionable to express some knowledge of leaders who are sociopaths, narcissists, and snakes in suits. Occasionally a rotten leader is abruptly identified and appears in a prime-time media venue reserved for corporate bad boys. Questions abound. Should an organization continue to invest in a toxic leader? Can a seemingly nasty university provost or dysfunctional CEO profit from the detoxification training of a leadership coach? Or will it require the swift removal of the rotten apple in order to eliminate the toxic source? Confronted with pressing problems of turnover, absenteeism, and grievances, can an organization turn to a leadership coach or management consultant for swift interventions and resolution?

Be prepared. The dark side of leadership requires unusual insight, savvy, and patience. Do not expect a seasoned management consultant or coach to neatly diagnose and exorcise a toxic leader from your organization. Such instances are fairly uncommon. Coaches and consultants will testify to the fact that corporate toxicity rarely has a single cause, leader, or culprit. Comparative negligence is a fact. Even the most toxic of leaders is interwoven within the workings of the organization. The broader system is inevitably in the mix. Most likely, a toxic leader is embedded in a dysfunctional organization housing deviance, poor policies, avoidance behavior, and a negligent approach to social intelligence, team building, and collaboration. Any attempts at isolating Kenneth Lay and Jeff Skilling from Enron, of separating Dennis Kozlowski from Tyco, or of disconnecting Bernard Madoff from a brokerage firm and numerous players affiliated with his Ponzi scheme are doomed to naïveté and failure. Destructive leaders require investors, followers, and a supportive and sustainable network of true believers and toxic cohorts seeded throughout the organization.

Perhaps you are curious about how to handle a toxic leader or have had experience with one. Are you presently concerned enough to explore your organization's readiness to deal with destructive leadership? Have you addressed downside protection? Here I intend to illuminate the workings of toxicity to the extent that you will consider moving forward and addressing the darker side of leaders. I am confident that you will see elements of yourself and your organization in the consulting cases presented in this book. As the inevitability of toxic behavior becomes increasingly apparent, the need to address bad leadership turns into a high-level priority. How do you proceed? Are your human resource people up to the task? Do they have adequate training and experience in clinical psychology, psychopathology, leadership, and relationship building to really hone in on toxic behavior? Are managers sufficiently trained and empowered as toxin detectors and toxin healers? Does your business stress relationship, communication, and people skills in annual workplace appraisals of leaders? Have you considered the prospects for more closely and systematically monitoring the soft-tissue or relationship side of your workplace? How much thought has been given to developing internal coaching and consulting to promote and sustain positive teamwork and leaders? Do you sufficiently value successful collaboration and authentic, visionary leadership?

DETAILED NARRATIVES AND THICK DESCRIPTIONS

In this book I answer these questions by ushering you into a world of toxic leaders and organizations. I am committed to immersing you in something more than the usual array of metrics, theories, and sound-bite versions of destructive leaders. Here you will find detailed narratives and thick descriptions of organizational culture, conflict, communication breakdowns, and struggles to locate the nexus of toxicity and do something about it. In serving as a coach I sometimes find myself untangling and debriefing organizations that have been traumatized by leaders through poorly conceived or clandestine versions of 360-degree feedback (see glossary). As the external expert I am at times called upon to work with companies to sort through the efforts of a previous consultant who was manipulated by a toxic leader to generate skewed data. Extremely bright executives are quite capable of manipulating their external experts and spreading their toxicity throughout the organization.

By sharing stories of function and dysfunction I hope to create a qualitative data base that extends our conversation and provides deeper insight into the many faces of toxicity. Ultimately, by the close of this book, I trust you will be closer to accurately recognizing toxicity and understanding the preventive measures that an organization can take. Moreover, there may be reason to consider employing external management consultants and leadership coaches to extend an organization's detoxification and recovery repertoire. I describe the positive concepts, strategies, and actions that can be utilized in day-to-day operations. In the final chapter I examine how leader toxicity presents both serious challenges and unprecedented opportunity for organizational development and growth. At times there is a fine line between trauma and renewal, crisis and rejuvenation, negative and positive deviance, and deficit and abundance gaps.

TOXIC LEADERS ARE DIFFICULT TO DETECT

As the consultant and coach I provide an insider's view of classified corporate operations and struggles. It is an exercise in making the invisible visible. In the following pages I open the previously closed corporate doors of Bentley Pacific, North Country Solutions, SkyWaves Aerospace, Eisenhower Heart Institute, Jarling-Weber Inc., and EuroText International to reveal the intricacies and complexities of toxic leaders and dysfunctional organizations. Toxic leaders may be quite difficult to detect. They are frequently protected by their followers and corporate brethren. They typically do not act alone. They are empowered by, fueled by, and serve as players in webs of destructive behavior populated by colleagues, executive boards, policy makers, customers, and stakeholders. Productivity, profits, and quarterly reports rule. The quality of human relationships is swept aside. Emotional intelligence becomes a footnote, an afterthought. Greed and power plays emerge.

There are many complex organizational scenarios conducive to the high incidence of toxic leaders. In Chapter 3 I tell the story of a human resources (HR) director who looks the other way while a heart surgeon has repeated angry exchanges with his surgical team. The threat of death-by-surgery and medical malpractice is unattended to and escalates daily. A few members of the surgeon's team filed grievances against him, banding together to make their leader look as bad as possible. Eisenhower executives initially bought into this "fish rots from the head down" routine and greeted an external leadership coach with the assessment that "the doctor is guilty as charged." But the consultants looked beyond the client's incomplete internal assessment and provided a differential diagnosis (see glossary) of the dysfunctional cardiology division; they resisted the client's indictment and ostracizing of the surgeon.

The morality plays at stake shed light on basic truths inseparable from power, competition, destructive coalitions, and the difficulty of unraveling truth within a complex organizational system. Single, simple causality is for simple minds. Multiple causality is what the consultant typically uncovers—even when all client roads and assessments appear to point toward a solo toxic source.

TALKING SHOP

Talking shop is all about bringing outsiders into the field and firing line of real-time consulting and coaching assignments and providing you with an insider's vantage point. I speak to multiple professional audiences: upper echelon corporate leaders and executive boards; managers and HR directors; leadership coaches and management consultants; organizational behavior, leadership, psychology, and human communication scholars, as well as their MBA and doctoral students; and a litany of intelligent readers who are on a quest to unravel troubling human behavior in high places.

I see myself as an action researcher engaged with leaders and immersed in client organizations, doing work not unlike that conducted by anthropologists. In describing conflicts, destructive behavior, and toxic leadership, I attempt to also include strategic nuance and detail central to the unfolding psychological and organizational theater. At times I am in the middle of the action and allow the organizational drama to speak for itself.

Worth mentioning is a core distinction made by theorists in neighboring research streams. Under the heading of "organizational misbehavior" (OMB, see glossary) it has been stated that *OMB researchers limit themselves to assessing and studying only intentional misbehavior, not unintentional acts*. I wrestled long and hard with this distinction and find that it does not hold up for me. In consulting and coaching work I frequently find unruly and darkly complex motives entangled with organizational misbehavior. Surely toxic leaders harbor both intentional and unintentional motives. How do we draw the line between intentional and unintentional misbehavior and between low-level and high-level toxicity in our leaders? Certainly there are unscrupulous executives who fit the profile of the toxic snake in a suit whose behaviors are premeditated. They are motivated by greed and personal aggrandizement. But other leaders are driven by their brilliance and a dark underbelly of pathology not quite under their conscious control.

Perhaps because of my clinical psychology and psychotherapy background I am especially intrigued by those relatively "good bosses" who incorporate significant degrees of unintentionally toxic behavior. For example, among leaders diagnosed with attention deficit disorder (ADD) and attention-deficit/hyperactivity disorder (ADHD) (see glossary), I have often found that their abrasive, hyperactive, and frequently demeaning behavior with colleagues is largely unintentional and not under their conscious control. Research currently under way in the neuroscience of leadership holds some promise for better understanding some of the hardwiring of psychological afflictions and disorders that lead to unintentionally toxic behavior. For example, in this book you will find several references to leaders who I suspected might be suffering from intermittent explosive disorder (see glossary), and that that might be the source of their hurtful behavior. In other words, some leaders are not significantly in control of their own emotions and lack adequate ability to censor public displays of affection, grief, or anger.

Under clinical supervision, leaders suffering from depression, intermittent explosive disorder, antisocial personality disorder, or narcissistic personality disorder can substantially improve and go through a detoxification process (see Chapter 6). Accordingly, woven throughout the narratives you will find clinical interpretations and questions pertaining to the need for a bona fide psychological diagnosis of allegedly toxic leaders grounded in the *Diagnostic and Statistical Manual of the American Psychiatric Association* (DSM IV-TR) (see glossary). The lack of an ability to make an internal DSM IV-TR diagnosis may represent a significant shortcoming in attempting to assess toxic leadership behavior. Central is the organizational readiness and the ability of managers-as-counselors to include toxicity in their everyday repertoires. Along these lines, it behooves supervisors and human resource professionals to function as toxin detectors and handlers on the firing line.

In addition, the employee assistance program (EAP) may be the corporation's only internal entity trained and qualified to diagnose psychological disorders. Assuming that a leader does in fact warrant a DSM IV-TR diagnosis, this in turn becomes confidential or privileged information unless the leader/client is identified as a danger to self (DTS) or a danger to others (DTO) in the workforce. As will be revealed in these pages, the organization's repertoire of responses to an allegedly difficult or toxic leader will rest with this critical determination—a verdict that can be a serious point of healing or contention.

Overall, expanding and enhancing an organization's repertoire for assessment of toxicity is a major step in the right direction. Managers, leaders, consultants, coaches, and researchers can profit from a broad-based interdisciplinary approach to human behavior in the workplace. I urge you to be suspicious of simplistic causality and those who point toward a single source of organizational deviance. Entertain a broader approach and be open to a differential diagnosis—whether it is achieved inside your organization or through the expertise of an external consultant. A counselor consultant should be patient and humane, earn employees' trust, be a good listener, solicit detailed narratives from colleagues and subordinates, conduct extensive interviews that include anecdotal information, and work on the assumption that many destructive behaviors and relationships in the workplace require time and curiosity to unravel. Leaders should strive to enter into dialogue with experts from a variety of perspectives that can shed light on the broad range of leadership and workplace behavior. Superior leaders, coaches, and consultants conduct far-reaching searches for information and often benefit from professional and innovative partnerships with experts in such areas as: organizational behavior; strategy; projects management; leadership; industrial and organizational psychology; management consulting; executive coaching; psychotherapy; and counseling psychology. As a practitioner and scholar I combine an eclectic array of disciplines and perspectives in clinical leadership coaching, management consulting, and organizational therapy.

I invite you to join me in what I trust will be an interesting and sometimes intriguing inside look at companies on the brink, organizations in confusion and decline, corporations unaware of incipient toxicity, upper echelon leaders in search of a voice, the transformation of organizational deficits into abundance, and the turning of leader toxicity into opportunity.

In compliance with client privilege and confidentiality requirements central to counseling psychology, coaching, and consulting I have changed the names of the leaders, officers, players, and organizations whose stories appear in this book.

Note that throughout the text I use quotation marks liberally as a means of quoting and paraphrasing snippets of actual conversations and dialogues with clients and calling attention to the tone and type of language involved in sometimes bizarre, difficult, and emotionally laden communication.

Preview: A Blueprint for Transforming Toxic Leaders

Toxicity is a fact of corporate life. In the midst of our best efforts at visionary leadership we stumble upon the troubling, dark, and destructive side of human behavior. In *Transforming Toxic Leaders*, I open privileged clients' doors to unveil the struggles of organizations with misbehavior and the clandestine. The six cases presented here are interwoven with critical management theory and research.

In Figure 1, "Toxicity Dimensions: From Deficits to Opportunity," I provide a blueprint for the six cases. Notice as you read horizontally across Figure 1 that leaders and organizations are initially assessed as dysfunctional and through management consulting and leadership coaching they are moved into a normative range. Extraordinarily successful consultations go beyond reaching normative leadership and organizational performance and ultimately move toward superior performance.

In Figure 2, "Toxicity Continuum," I show five dimensions of leadership and organizational behavior ranging from the extremely dysfunctional to the super-functional. Figure 2 visually represents a core theme of the book: highly toxic leadership behavior may point an organization not only toward detoxification and normalization but also in the direction of superior performance. A core question is whether leader and organizational toxicity can motivate management toward progressively superior performance—that is, from deficits to opportunity and abundance.

Corporate Client	Client Reports of Symptoms and Deficits	Coach/Consultant's Differential Diagnosis and Assessment
Bentley Pacific *Cal Burton, CEO*	Grievances; turnover; insubordination; lost productivity; escalating absenteeism	Coercive downsizing; leader demagoguery; emotionally unintelligent CEO; relationship-deficient organizational policies and operations
North Country Solutions *Lane Blake, CEO*	Highly functional CEO identifies deficiencies in her leadership for possible coaching	Highly functional CEO in quest of leadership development and organizational excellence
SkyWaves Aerospace *Kathy Warner, HR Head*	Escalating anger issues in R&D engineering; high transfer rate of engineers; plunging productivity; faltering R&D	Chronic, long-term avoidance behavior from HR director and R&D head; high-level emotional unintelligence
Eisenhower Heart Institute, Phase 1 *Dr. Ivan Lorimer, Director, Cardiology*	Malpractice threat; anger management issues in cardiology department centered in director, Dr. Ivan Lorimer; legal threat from internal grievances	High toxicity threat from Dr. Lorimer's operating team during stress of open-heart surgeries; agitated Dr. Lorimer; faltering organizational restructuring
Jarling-Weber *Max Lunger, Senior Manager*	Lazy employees; employee insubordination; grievances filed; false psychological claims; dysfunctional diagnoses by EAP	Companywide post-traumatic stress; employee burnout; traumatized leader reluctantly playing hatchet man for upper echelon leadership
EuroText *David Gravestone, Manager*	Employee mutiny and group level insubordination toward senior manager	Leader suffering from high-level family and organizational stressors temporarily and unofficially withdrawing from duties; absentee leadership
Eisenhower Heart Institute, Phase 2 *Dr. Marshall Portello, CEO;* *Dr. Ivan Lorimer, Director 1;* *Dr. Avi Zaroff, Director 2*	Success of Phase 1 led Eisenhower client to aspire to shift out of normalization and into super-functional leadership with Dr. Lorimer as the center of operations	Developmental coaching and organizational consultation reveals prospect for expanding cardiology and reinventing Dr. Lorimer's leadership role in operations

Figure 1 Toxicity Dimensions: From Deficits to Opportunity

Toxicity Reports	Intervention	Strategy for Transforming Toxicity into Opportunity
Dysfunctional/toxic CEO behavior escalating to extremely dysfunctional/highly toxic; toxicity supported by upper echelon leadership	Differential diagnosis of organization; leadership coaching	Transform destructive downsizing into constructive downsizing
Highly functional CEO and positive organizational behavior throughout system; trace toxicity levels	Developmental leadership coaching	Transform highly functional CEO with trace-level toxicity into super-functional, super-positive organizational leader
44 engineer transfers in R&D over 6 years = highly toxic organizational behavior; toxic avoidance behavior; "no emotions allowed" company culture	Belated, ninth-inning intervention due to late call; differential diagnosis of organizational system; leadership coaching	Detoxify R&D engineering; install early toxin detection and handling; elevate emotional intelligence, emotional competence; promote relationship-rich workplace
Extremely dysfunctional surgical team with Dr. Lorimer one player in multiple causality; high-level companywide toxicity resulting from poor restructuring	Differential diagnosis; leadership coaching for Dr. Lorimer; consultations with HR director; detoxification of the restructuring; reduction in leadership duties of Dr. Lorimer	Immediate, short-range opportunity to detoxify and normalize cardiology department, surgical teams, and Dr. Lorimer; detoxify restructuring
Extremely dysfunctional/highly toxic system, and leadership; widespread post-traumatic stress syndrome; extreme client denial and resistance to consultant's recommended approach	Differential diagnosis; process consultation; action research; systemwide detoxification; leadership coaching; examination of EAP	System entropy and death imminent; leader coaching for detoxification; leader renewal via resignation and new career pathways
Bordering on extremely high leader toxicity levels; absentee leader with erratic behavior triggering employee agitation	Leadership coaching for ailing senior manager Gravestone; innovation of dual leadership	Opportunity for Gravestone recovery; dual leadership provides detoxification and opportunity for growth and development
Low, manageable toxicity levels after Phase 1 (above); functional cardiology operations striving for excellence or super-functional status	Hiring of Dr. Avi Zaroff, former colleague of Dr. Lorimer; restructuring of cardiology division with dual leadership	Dual leadership freed Dr. Lorimer to excel in surgical procedures and in collaboration with Dr. Zaroff to transform Eisenhower into a center for excellence

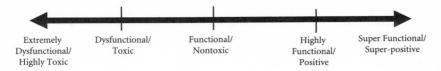

Figure 2   Toxicity Continuum

Transforming Toxic Leaders

1 Demagogue to Dialogue

Bentley Pacific Engineering and
North Country Solutions

*Like the two-faced Roman god, Janus, the leader must always
be looking both inwards and outwards, a difficult position . . .
concentrating solely on one or the other is a more comfortable
position but it undermines the role of the leader, and thus the
strength of the institution's representation in the outer world.*

—A. Obholzer, *The Unconscious at Work*

DYSFUNCTIONAL DOWNSIZING INC.: BENTLEY PACIFIC

Late one Friday afternoon as engineers and staff were about to depart for the
weekend, an e-mail terminating 273 employees suddenly appeared on monitors
throughout Bentley Pacific Engineering, a firm based in Seattle, Washington.
(As noted in the Introduction, I have changed the names of companies and individuals throughout the book to maintain client confidentiality and personal
privacy.) Shock waves of disbelief welled up as deeply committed aerospace de-
signers and administrative assistants attempted to grasp the full brunt of their
dismissals. They were to pack up their belongings and move out of their offices
before the start of the next workweek. The traumatic effect of the downsizing
extended beyond those terminated to the remaining employees, who assumed
that they would be next. Their colleagues had been the victims of a sudden act
of organizational sabotage. How could they ever trust leadership again?

Monday afternoon in a hastily called meeting, Bentley CEO Cal Burton
gave an obligatory, politically correct speech hitting on all of the cost-containment buttons. Burton's speech was an act of shallow showmanship, pure cliché,
and only served to deepen his employees' wounds and mistrust. It was all about
bottom lines, with no discussion of human capital or recognition of the emotion of his audience. Immediately following the CEO's talk, twelve managers
informed members of their respective divisions that the downsizing was still
in progress, with further cuts inevitable. Meanwhile, both professionals and

staff received an edict that they would be expected to rise to the occasion and perform at 125 to 150 percent of their usual levels in an effort to make up for the losses in productivity anticipated after the downsizing.

When the new rules of the game were questioned by angry and traumatized engineers, divisional managers were directed by CEO Burton to put down any rebellion by whatever means necessary. A number of verbal altercations occurred throughout the company, highlighted by a screaming and pushing match involving Burton and three remaining engineers from the R&D division. Grievances were filed against the CEO, with litigation pending. Further investigation involving consultation with the Bentley employee assistance program (EAP) director and an external management consulting group yielded that Burton was an easily agitated man for whom tantrum-style outbursts were not uncommon. His anger issues and temper resulted in increasingly turbulent behavior in the workplace.

PSYCHOLOGICAL ASSESSMENT OF THE CEO

The consultants collectively considered whether Burton's individual behavioral patterns could be untangled and separated from the painful realities of a downsizing. Perhaps the downsizing was the true cause of all the Bentley conflict and agony? Clearly, companywide policies and unpopular but necessary fiscal decisions were major drivers of a dysfunctional system. Discussions determined that since there was no way of neatly separating a leader from the organizational system it made good sense to isolate Burton as the lowest-hanging fruit in this corporate debacle. All roads appeared to lead back to Burton. Why not determine whether he was the nexus of the crisis and do something about it?

After much deliberation, the Huntington-Bolger Management Consulting Group in conjunction with the Bentley EAP concluded that Burton's issues required more in-depth mental and emotional assessment, and he was referred to Dr. Alexander Silverton, a leadership coach with a unique combination of management and clinical psychology expertise. Faced with a growing avalanche of grievances and lawsuits, both Bentley Pacific and the Huntington-Bolger Group were hopeful that individual leadership coaching and psychological assessment of Burton could yield insights into some companywide damage control. After three weeks of extensive coaching and assessment, Dr. Silverton reached a DSM IV-TR diagnosis of intermittent explosive disorder (American Psychiatric Association 2000, pp. 663–67; also see glossary). Apparently, Burton had both a brilliant and a dark history as a leader who was a mover and shaker, a CEO who was able to pull a company out of the dumps and into almost overnight profitability—but at the serious cost of demeaning and traumatizing scores of subordinates. With a fiercely hierarchical and authoritarian leadership style, Burton had a reputation as a mercenary and soldier of fortune; he had served as a "downsizing shark" and a "one-man cost-containment militia" for five companies over the previous twelve years. Curiously, Burton's predisposition to extreme, exaggerated, and repetitive public displays of anger had been painfully apparent to a growing number of colleagues at Bentley Pacific, but the official diagnosis was not revealed to the company by Dr. Silverton. Although Dr. Silverton was hired by Bentley Pacific via a referral, Burton was legally protected by confidentiality and privileged communication provisions of the Americans with Disabilities Act as it applies to psychological and psychiatric diagnoses.

Burton continued with his leadership coach and eventually resumed his full-time duties as Bentley's practicing CEO. Since Dr. Silverton did not diagnose Burton as being either a danger to self (DTS) or a danger to others (DTO), he was given clearance to resume his duties as CEO, pending additional and ongoing treatment.

TOXIC LEADERSHIP

But a dark cloud engulfed Bentley Pacific. Owing to the privileged status of Burton's coaching and treatment by Dr. Silverton, the company returned to the status quo. Management was once again intimidated and confused by Burton, and publicly did its best to follow the CEO's marching orders. The ultimatum from management was clear: employees would have to expand their work hours into evenings and weekends or risk receiving an updated version of the "Black Friday" e-mail. The only compensation promised was the slim prospect of holding on to a position in the midst of a bleak job market. It was a strategy of pure intimidation and negative reinforcement.

The organizational pain permeating Bentley Pacific was to a significant degree due to toxic leadership at the top. In extreme situations where mass downsizings may be justifiable, only a minority of leaders gradually and sensitively break the news to their employees (Cameron 1994; Cameron and Lavine 2006; Goldman 2007). Not only was Bentley Pacific leadership the bearer of dreadfully bad news, but because he was so sorely lacking in people skills or any semblance of social or emotional intelligence, the pain caused by the firings was even more devastating than it might have been (Goleman 1995, 2000). Under the toxic leadership of Cal Burton, the downsizing proceeded in a devious, secretive, and treacherous fashion, eliminating 198 employees and destroying any trust that remained among those who had been spared. Thoughts of retaliation loomed large among the wounded engineers and staff.

Meanwhile, Dr. Silverton continued to work in the trenches as CEO Burton's coach and organizational therapist (see Schein 2005). Slow to detect that the CEO might require special attention in the form of leadership coaching, the consultants had made their referral fairly late—limiting the organization's chances for damage control, healing, or transformation. By the time Dr. Silverton reached a diagnosis, little could be done to lighten the load of the downsizing or decrease the swell of grievances or lawsuits. And the ADA's requirements of privileged communication surrounding DSM diagnoses limited both Dr. Silverton's and Bentley Pacific's options. The diagnosis could not legally be revealed to the company. Members of the Bentley Pacific board of directors and the head of human resources (HR) intuitively suspected that Burton had "gone postal," but there was little they could do about it other than place their faith in Dr. Silverton. From a larger perspective, however, the explosive personality of Burton was reflected in the totalitarian strategy of the Bentley downsizing. Although the grievances and lawsuits were not anticipated, the ironclad leadership deemed necessary to effect a massive, overnight downsizing was in fact characteristic of Bentley Pacific's management style. Burton delivered a harsh edict, perhaps too harsh even for Bentley's extreme theory X (authoritarian) objectives (see glossary). Several of the Bentley old-school hard-liners whispered that perhaps Burton had gone too far.

FUNCTIONAL DOWNSIZING INC.: NORTH COUNTRY SOLUTIONS

In sharp contrast, the leaders of the nearby Vancouver, British Columbia–based engineering company and competitor, North Country Solutions, handled their downsizing in a radically different fashion. North Country's CEO, Lane Blake, was deeply influenced by her direct knowledge of the heralded and highly successful downsizing at Rocky Flats Nuclear Plant in Denver, Colorado (see Cameron and Lavine 2006). Blake believed that the forward-thinking leaders of Rocky Flats had been instrumental in pointing the way for other organizations to minimize the organizational pain of a wide-scale termination. Lane Blake was committed to a systemwide cooperative and relationship-building approach to radical organizational transformation. A pivotal point in her "kinder, sweeter downsizing" was Ms. Blake's decision to spend six months preparing her targeted professionals for the financial dilemma confronting North Country Solutions. In a series of face-to-face meetings with the engineers most likely to be released, Lane Blake and five members of her management team explained at length the possible employment ramifications of the "difficult North Country drama" that was unfolding.

Following the CEO's vision, the management team operated as managerial counselors and internal coaches (see Whetten and Cameron 2007) and carefully addressed the affective and emotional dimensions of the tough times ahead. Blake and her associates spent many hours delving into the individual concerns and fears of each employee and preparing them for a career transition in the foreseeable future. Supportive communication, empathy, and resilience in the face of the downsizing preoccupied the managerial team (see Bright, Cameron, and Caza 2006; Fineman 1996; Frederickson 2003). Despite the ensuing cuts, leadership was determined to make it right with the engineers. The CEO-led team personalized the process and attempted to turn threats into opportunities and weaknesses into strengths (see Clifton and Harter 2003). Blake conceived of the imminent parting of ways as "but a hill or small mountain that a business family must climb as they face the challenges of growing up and apart." Along these lines Blake decided to make transparent to her engineers the financial hardships driving the downsizing. Blake believed that making the targeted engineers privy to the hard data would be a step en route to facilitating trust and constructive dialogue (Burke 2002). In addition, the CEO was committed to preparing the exiting engineers for the outside world and professional life after North Country. Those being terminated were provided with extensive training and retraining options accompanied by one-on-one coaching to address networking, introductions to prospective employers, and job searches. Whenever possible, the downsized engineers were placed on a short list of employees to be potentially rehired as North Country outside contractors (without benefits).

The humane downsizing approach at North Country Solutions emerged from a culture of collaboration and empowerment, in contrast to the culture of avoidance and demagoguery at Bentley Pacific. The relationship-oriented leadership extended to a careful articulation with remaining North Country employees who feared for their jobs. CEO Blake and associates made it abundantly clear that the company was ready to stand by their remaining employees to the bitter end. They were assured that their jobs were safe as long as North Country was able to survive and fend off the growing threat of a hostile takeover by either Bentley Pacific or the Toronto conglomerate Maple Leaf Aeronautics. North Country guaranteed their continued employment for the life of the organization and also provided them with an incentive-based partnership whereby strong performance was linked to generous financial rewards (see Lawler 2000).

DEMAGOGUE TO DIALOGUE

On the surface, the leadership of both Bentley Pacific and North Country Solutions dealt with the unpleasant task of a companywide downsizing of high-level professionals. As revealed, however, CEOs Burton and Blake conceived of and approached their downsizings in dramatically different fashion. The North Country strategy of empowering and including both the exiting and the remaining engineers in a substantive dialogue softened the impending threat and made a typically top-down decision into a more humane and empowering affair. The functional relationship approach yielded a 93 percent placement rate for the terminated engineers into either new professional appointments or as independent contractors for North Country. Of 212 employees directly affected by the downsizing, only two filed grievances against North Country. The two disputes were eventually satisfactorily resolved through the collective and collaborative efforts of the human resources department, the in-house EAP, and an external consultant working with CEO Lane Blake.

In contrast, the Bentley Pacific downsizing was met with extensive in-house grievances and twenty-seven lawsuits vigorously pursued in the courts, resulting in a further corporate financial drain and deteriorating image management. According to one of the legal transcripts from a Bentley Pacific engineer,

> The Bentley Pacific downsizing is a grave disappointment to me, and I speak as a dedicated eleven-year veteran of this company. But it is not the mass firing that brings me to the point of a grievance and determined legal action. It is the condescending, patronizing, and despicable manner in which I was terminated. The CEO and my immediate division head, Elton Blackwell, never did prepare me or warn me face-to-face. It was all secretive . . . an ambush . . . an act of sabotage against your own people. I've even heard that the CEO has some kind of psychiatric condition. How dysfunctional can you get? When you treat your engineers as expendable widgets you can expect some backlash. Engineers have some blood and pride flowing through their veins . . . at least I do, last time I checked.

The emotionally explosive, top-down handling of the Bentley Pacific downsizing escalated its negative impact and set the stage for deterioration and confrontation. Faced with resistance and a groundswell of conflict, a CEO with a dysfunctional past turned an already bad situation increasingly toxic.

Anger and physical disputes appeared to emanate from CEO Cal Burton consistent with his longstanding problems with an intermittent explosive disorder. Toxicity took a grip on the organizational culture when a series of verbal and physical altercations arose at Bentley Pacific. The disruptive downsizing morphed into widespread bullying, intimidation, and physically destructive acts. Overly trusting in the newly anointed CEO as a heroic leader and corporate savior, Bentley Pacific unwittingly set the stage for a demagogue. CEO Burton's explosive outbursts agitated both his management team and a significant percentage of the engineers. The revelation of his darker side during the stressful downsizing resulted in widespread negative deviance among the employees.

In contrast, Lane Blake enjoyed considerable success with her approach to the North Country downsizing. Dr. Irene Daniels served as Blake's confidant and leadership coach. Daniels prepared Blake for the streamlining by systematically examining approximately forty-five cases of western European, Canadian, and U.S. corporate downsizings, with special scrutiny on successes and failures. Best practices of analogous companies were identified (e.g., Rocky Flats Nuclear Plant), and various scenarios were discussed in the context of the North Country organizational culture. As a caveat, Blake was well schooled in a more theory Y, or participatory, approach to her workforce, a horizontal and empowerment approach that was compatible with companies benchmarked in her research with Daniels (see theory Y and theory X in the glossary). Of particular concern to Blake were the people skills required in breaking bad news and the importance of nurturing and maintaining a dialogue through the most troubling of times. Blake had already developed an emotionally intelligent, relationship-building approach to workplace conflict, but had to apply this to the specific objectives and potential pitfalls of a downsizing. The trials and tribulations of downsizings were aptly covered by Dr. Daniels, who brought direct knowledge of radical organizational transformation to her client. Via role playing, case studies, simulations, and scenarios, Daniels and Blake worked through a myriad of contingencies and approaches to the downsizing, conceiving of it as a complex, systemwide objective.

Blake was not hesitant to reveal her fears, doubts, and insecurities to Dr. Daniels. Although she had had many successes at North Country, there had also been some troublesome communication breakdowns with engineers and repeated minor conflicts and "brushfires." In the words of Dr. Daniels, "there were a few blind spots that required illumination." Even the carefully conceived and strategized North Country downsizing put both terminated and surviving employees on edge and made many fearful, angry, and confrontational. In coaching sessions Blake further revealed that she occasionally "felt driven by the numbers, manhandled by the executive board, and pushed against the wall to create fiscal miracles and show quarterly earnings far beyond what reality allotted." When she felt pressure from above, Blake admitted that she could be impatient, hurried, frazzled, and abrupt in her decision-making. As she became increasingly aware of these tendencies through coaching, Blake worked with Dr. Daniels on maintaining a more balanced style of leadership, including an ability to focus on small wins and no longer succumbing to the mental and emotional state of being overwhelmed. As a leader, Blake was deeply influenced by what Dr. Daniels called the Rocky Flats–inspired "quest to make the impossible possible." Blake wanted to take her ability to function as a successful leader to the higher ground of "extraordinary leadership."

LEADERSHIP UNDER FIRE: FROM TOXIC TO EXTRAORDINARY

Destructive behavior in leaders negatively affects the loyalty, productivity, motivation, health, and happiness of employees (Kellerman 2004; Pfeffer and Sutton 2006). Fortune 500 firms are increasingly recognizing this dark side of leadership as a reality of organizational life. Some leaders enter organizations with a history of narcissism, bullying behavior, and rage. In the case of Cal Burton, his intermittent explosive disorder was in part beyond his rational control and presented Bentley Pacific with *unintended* toxicity. Unfortunately, Burton's bad behavior surfaced in the context of a downsizing, providing further impetus for a negative employee reaction. Ironically, Burton's condescending and explosive approach was initially condoned and empowered by the Bentley board of directors as befitting a hostile situation. According to longstanding Bentley Pacific culture, the abrupt elimination of employees required unwavering theory X–style leadership. Members of the executive board found Burton's loud and bullying behavior "quite humorous" and "long overdue in a company of lazy and spoiled engineers." They did not expect the deluge of grievances and lawsuits that were filed against the company.

As a result, Bentley Pacific's board began a line of questioning surrounding how to promptly exercise damage control and prevent similar catastrophes. The grievances and lawsuits presented a pattern: they were focused primarily on Burton, and secondarily on Bentley as a company. Bentley Pacific recognized that the distasteful task of downsizing had turned seriously toxic under Burton's leadership. Moreover, because the bad news of the mass firing had been mishandled, the fear factor metastasized throughout the workforce. The remaining employees had a difficult time functioning, and the disastrous situation was bringing the company to its knees. Questions abounded. What led to the massive organizational dysfunction, and how had Cal Burton's leadership directly affected the downward spiral?

At North Country Solutions, in contrast, CEO Lane Blake preserved a relatively positive workplace demeanor during a very troubled time. Bentley Pacific quietly looked over its shoulder at North Country and wondered what could be learned from the Canadians. Faced with a difficult cost-containment dilemma, can a leader rise to the occasion and make the most out of a seemingly bad situation? Burton failed and Blake succeeded. Perhaps a prototype could be derived from Blake's leadership?

Fortune 500s learn from painful downsizings. Part of this learning process is to review presuppositions and values and to enter into a questioning mode involving the seeking of alternatives to the alpha male's methods of demagoguery and intimidation. The in-your-face authoritarian approach utilized at Bentley Pacific only served to accentuate the pain of disrupted livelihoods, derailed careers, and painful divorces from a company. At stake is more than a mere approach to leadership in the face of a downsizing. The surprisingly *positive deviance* of North Country points toward the unfolding of a leadership and organizational prototype. We can deeply appreciate the lessons implicit in a corporate culture that turns adversity into advantage and threat into opportunity.

The positive mindset and strategy of CEO Lane Blake begs for dissection. Curiously, the success of Blake was only a stepping stone for the North Country CEO. As a strong performer who aspired to extraordinary leadership, Blake frequently repeated her belief in "the vision thing" to Dr. Daniels. The CEO's overriding objective throughout her work with Daniels was to transition from a "merely strong leader" into a truly superior and transformational leader "able to fill her employees with a deeply motivating vision and purpose." Dr. Daniels assured Lane Blake that the ability to develop and instill positive organizational behaviors (POBs) during the trauma of a downsizing would provide her with some of the most essential building blocks for blossoming into an extraordinary leader. Daniels meticulously coached Blake in positive organizational behavior and psychological capital (see Nelson and Cooper 2007; Luthans, Youssef, and

Avolio 2007a, 2007b). The development of self-efficacy, hope, optimism, and resilience were identified as cornerstones of extraordinary achievement, Everest heights, and "abundance leadership" (Cameron and Lavine 2006) (see Everest goals and abundance leadership in the glossary).

On the other hand, Bentley Pacific suffered at the hands of CEO Burton and entered into its downsizing without adequate preparation. The organization had little understanding of European and North American companies that had already laid down a track record of the good, the bad, and the ugly. Lacking at Bentley Pacific was an adequate understanding of the mental and emotional state of Cal Burton. Under the pressure of an ill-conceived downsizing, Burton's longstanding explosive behavior came out of remission and into the forefront. Left lurking was the difficult proposition of how to screen, assess, anticipate, coach, and ultimately transform a toxic leader. Certainly anything short of a resourceful, resilient, and emotionally competent leader is not in a position to handle an organizational change agenda as trying as a companywide downsizing. With the benefit of hindsight, I wonder whether organizations and leaders can learn from the toxic treatment of Bentley employees orchestrated by Burton. Can the toxic behavior of a leader serve as an impetus or a springboard for positive personal and organizational transformation?

At the heart of this book is the premise that the dark side and the most trying moments of leadership can provide a formidable stimulus for innovation and positive transformation. In the best outcome they can "make the impossible possible."

TOXIC LEADERS ARE ENTRENCHED IN THEIR COMPANIES

It is not a simple matter to spot the rotten apple in the barrel. Beyond doubt, the screening system at Bentley Pacific did not have a 360-degree view of Cal Burton when he was hired. There was considerable failure and even negligence on the part of the executive recruitment consultants who vouched for the ability of Burton to provide strong, visionary leadership. A few companies who have been burned one time too many by executive recruiters are now subcontracting with external clinical psychologists to screen leadership candidates during the hiring process. Doing so requires even more than effort and skill to find the dark side of a potential hire. By turning to consultants with clinical psychology expertise, companies are hopeful that they will be able to create an additional filtering and early warning system for spotting potentially toxic upper echelon leaders.

Bentley's Cal Burton did in fact display some of the diabolical charms iden-tified by Babiak and Hare (2006) in their exposé on negative charismatics and psychologically unbalanced and unethical leaders. Burton's sophistication and allure made it difficult for the unsuspecting Bentley HR director, president, vice president, and members of the executive board to detect that he was a "snake in a suit." Despite the lengthy, multilevel interview process at Bentley Pacific, in the final analysis they empowered the external management search firm to select their next CEO.

Whether assessing couples, families, or organizations, insufficiently trained and inexperienced interviewers can have difficulty recognizing a troubled and destructive individual. Accordingly, there is a case to be made that corporations should have at least one human resource professional on board with advanced counseling or clinical psychology training. Second, there is a growing precedent for subcontracting with an external psychologist or psychotherapist to partici-pate in a multilevel interview of potential leaders. A growing list of organiza-tions can testify that once a dysfunctional leader gets past the entry portal and becomes part of your larger system, toxicity is inevitable.

For better or for worse, it is not unusual for a company to unwittingly in-ternalize and reproduce the personality and behavioral patterns of its CEO. Ac-cording to Dr. Silverton, the coach advising Cal Burton, "the Bentley corporate culture had gradually taken on the characteristics of the CEO's intermittent explosive disorder." Deeply entrenched at the core of the company, Burton's emotional turbulence and outbursts morphed into an insidious institutional virus. The intermittent explosive disorder seeped into the interpersonal and structural existence of the Bentley Pacific workplace. The ramifications of Bur-ton's destructive behavior loomed larger than life and set a toxic agenda for the entire organization. The CEO's explosiveness reverberated because he occupied a central role in the organization.

The leader, however, is not a solo agent. Leaders exist within organizations. Bentley Pacific served as the dysfunctional context and culture for Burton's toxic leadership. Burton exploded within a dysfunctional culture initially in-tent on fueling and condoning negative organizational behaviors (NOBs). As the CEO's leadership coach, Dr. Silverton explained, "Cal Burton was just what the doctor ordered for Bentley Pacific." Changing Burton's behavior, however, would not have significantly affected the Bentley approach to downsizing. In fact, Bentley's president and entourage had gone looking for a version of Sun-beam's Al "Chainsaw" Dunlap, and they found him in Cal Burton. Burton was never exactly cool under pressure. When the stress level went up, Burton became inflamed and over-reactive, and in the words of several middle managers, "he did a damn good impression of an earlier twentieth-century German dictator with a dark moustache." As a CEO who micromanaged by walking around, Burton was so extremely quick on the draw and hard hitting that there was little opportunity for a fired or disgruntled engineer to exact retribution by stealing files, implanting computer viruses, or spying for a competitor. The swift hit and eradication of employees actually suited the Bentley executive board and was precisely executed by Burton. But his explosive manner created a toxic downsizing far beyond what was anticipated.

2 Emotional Deposits and Withdrawals

SkyWaves Aerospace International

Whereas the Greeks viewed emotions as irrational animal passions that needed to be constrained, modern theories of emotions posit that emotions are adaptations that have important evolutionary functions that are critical to our survival.

—R. Lowman, ed., *Handbook of Organizational and Consulting Psychology*

I encounter much talk about the role of the emotions in leadership. Clients tell stories that veer off the main highway of analysis and are not always limited to the purely rational. At times it is quite awkward for a consultant to discuss with a CEO how the passions of the human animal are part and parcel of leadership. Even more discomforting is the search for some sign of affect or enthusiasm in the midst of what appears to be an emotionally barren corporate wasteland. As will be revealed in this chapter, the absence or denial of emotions in the workplace is reason for concern.

What are the consequences of leadership's emotional unintelligence? Can emotional deficits be transformed into assets? This chapter illustrates how a failure of leadership at SkyWaves Aerospace to respond in a timely manner to an emotionally volatile and threatening altercation between two engineers eventually morphed into companywide toxicity. Committed to a "leave your emotions at the door" policy, SkyWaves' leadership belittled attempts at relationship building and conflict resolution. Leadership and subordinates excelled at emotional withdrawal. Throughout the SkyWaves hierarchy, emotional bank accounts were gradually depleted and eventually overdrawn. Leadership was unavailable to respond to disturbing behavior among R&D engineers. Opportunities for resolution were closed or rendered inoperable. Unable to find a venue for dialogue or healing, the feuding engineers turned increasingly secretive and toxic.

Why have some organizations been slow to acknowledge the need for emotional competency? Why have leaders maintained an active resistance and adversarial posture toward any mention of the merits of emotional intelligence (EI)? For nearly twenty years emotional intelligence researchers have been putting leaders on notice regarding the limits of left-brain, logical, and analytical intelligence. But despite the recent groundbreaking work of Frost (2003) the message that "emotions at work" are inevitable continues to be met by resistance. A strong preference for "intellectual smarts" over "emotional smarts" still prevails in organizations.

Researchers and consultants have continued to push the EI message in corporate circles. Influenced by a wellspring of emotional intelligence publications and training programs, Fortune 500s treat emotions in the workplace, affirmative or toxic, as both formidable and contagious. When a CEO readily communicates compassion, anger, or aloofness, it rapidly spreads through the office space of JVC, American Express, Costco, Nissan, Disneyland Paris, and Honeywell. As a poster child for emotional intelligence in the workplace, Libby Sartain of Southwest Airlines was committed to growing a corporate culture of employees who exuded passion and established caring relationships with coworkers and customers (Sartain 2003). Emotional competency and a relationship-rich workplace reigned supreme at Southwest. In contrast, leadership at SkyWaves Aerospace sidestepped employee expressions of agitation, anger, and indignation, assuming a posture of disengagement and avoidance. Where Southwest made emotional deposits, SkyWaves Aerospace made emotional withdrawals. The hard business truths at SkyWaves were vested in the task-driven data and productivity measurables. People skills were beside the point. Metrics were the legal tender.

EMOTIONAL UNINTELLIGENCE AT SKYWAVES AEROSPACE

Over a three-year period, 22 percent of the engineers in the R&D division of SkyWaves Aerospace International had applied for a transfer. This once stable R&D division was known throughout the SkyWaves Aerospace global network as "the human turnstile." During this period of time, productivity dropped by one-third and profits plunged. Gossip reached all the way to the Amsterdam and Glasgow Euro-subsidiaries that "there was a psychodrama at SkyWaves headed by a few pathological engineers."

Kathy Warner, the new HR director, took notice of the toxic situation within approximately three months of assuming her position. At first glance Warner had observed hard-working, innovative engineers collaborating effectively in their think tanks. Further observation led to another view: the atmosphere in R&D was at times rude and disruptive. R&D had a reputation for productivity and high-level creativity, but there was also a darker and troubled side to the division. Warner was a bit baffled by the transfer data, but was even more concerned by the fact that the former HR leader, Melissa Jones-Seaver, had made no mention of personnel disturbances in R&D during their transition. Why did her predecessor not mention this problem? Was something being hidden? Avoided?

DEVELOPMENT OF THE INTERNAL TOXIN DETECTOR

Finally, opportunity knocked in the form of another transfer request. Lucas Frazier, a nine-year veteran of SkyWaves, sent through the necessary paperwork for a transfer to the Burlingame, California, location. Warner set up a "transfer interview," a first cousin of an exit interview, developed several years earlier owing to the high SkyWaves Aerospace transfer rate. Apparently a slew of grievances filed from the R&D division were resulting in transfers to other locations in SkyWaves' global network. Frazier responded to Warner's nonthreatening, personable line of questioning with candor. When asked what his reasons were for requesting the transfer, he replied with a story about "intolerable conflict, backbiting behavior, and a culture of intolerance and emotional terrorism." Warner patiently asked for some insight into how this culture of conflict all came about. Frazier complied by offering, "Here's the nasty story as I see it. Don't quote me, but it's pretty accurate."

For some five years there had been a "serious feud" between two senior cockpit engineers. David Cutter and Eugene McKenna had it in for each other. Several years earlier, HR director Jones-Seaver had responded by sending both McKenna and Cutter off to the EAP for psychological counseling. According to Frazier, she never said a word about the problem and spent little if any time with the two engineers. What about Julius Jefferson, the R&D division chief? Frazier colorfully commented, "Our illustrious leader was a nonfactor. He didn't buy into the whole people conflict, psychological thing. Jefferson is about work. If you had a human drama you went off to HR. And HR seemed to automatically send the rotten apples off to the EAP."

Talk seemed to leak out from the EAP. Or maybe they were just rumors. The word around the cockpit engineering people was that McKenna was "dangerously hostile." A few of the engineers gossiped that McKenna was a "manic depressive" and suffered from some kind of "personality disorder." Whatever the truth was, Frazier offered that the whole division had to tiptoe around these two "nut cases" as "there was no escape from this lethal feud. It never ended!" But what about Cutter? According to Frazier, Cutter was very introverted and appeared to be baiting McKenna. Frazier offered that it was well known that several engineers mocked Cutter behind the scenes, spreading gossip that he was a "pathetic passive-aggressive." But who really knew? Something was behind it all, and meanwhile everyone was suffering.

Warner dug deeper in order to determine whether Frazier's account was reliable. Warner learned that Frazier had been best friends with McKenna for many years but that they had recently had a falling out. Apparently McKenna was livid at Frazier for his attempt to intervene and act as a peacemaker in the six-year-old feud. As a result, Frazier was hurt, frustrated, and determined to get to the bottom of the conflict by coming forth to the new and amiable HR director, Warner.

Following up on the Frazier interview, Warner proceeded to individually interview all forty-four members of the R&D division. The gist of the narratives matched Frazier's recollection fairly closely. Finally, the smoking gun emerged when Warner sat down with McKenna. McKenna was ready to talk. He felt comfortable with Warner. What was the origin of all this toxic behavior and dysfunctional impact?

THE MANAGER AS INTERNAL COACH AND TOXIN HANDLER

Approximately six years earlier Cutter had made an allegedly highly insulting public statement about McKenna's father, who had just died from a brain aneurysm. The statement instantly caused loss of face to McKenna since it was uttered at a large divisional meeting at SkyWaves Aerospace. McKenna recalled that he had recently spent the worst weeks of his life living through a botched surgery and a family tragedy that struck him very hard. Despite it all, McKenna only took off four days from work and continued to come in and do his best to be innovative and helpful to his work team. Warner was more than a little surprised to find out that McKenna had carried these unexpressed emotions with him for six years and never had a face-to-face discussion with Cutter about them. Even more surprising was what McKenna revealed to Warner:

> I was totally uncomfortable telling this to anyone in the company. I'd never tell that former HR lady or ever tell Jefferson. They would just mock me. Check your emotions in at the door. The workplace is not for confessionals. No emo-

tions allowed! Besides, if you dared talk about people conflicts, that would automatically kick me up to the funny farm . . . you know, EAP. I certainly am not buying into that tar pit.

Returning to his assessment of Cutter, the object of his venom, McKenna labeled Cutter a "passive aggressive" and "psycho" who "tried to set me up to freak out and look wacko in front of my team." Questioned whether other workers shared McKenna's assessment, he whispered,

> Yeah, plenty of engineers knew the story. Not that they were truly interested . . . but they knew what was going on. I probably shouldn't have, but I let some of my colleagues know that Cutter's a psycho passive-aggressive. Look, if I didn't brief them on his disturbances then they'd turn around and think I'm the one who's unbalanced. I was just dealing in the trenches with a colleague who had a contract . . . a vendetta out on me . . . in his troubled head. Besides, I have my connections upstairs in the EAP. I got sources.

Clearly there was a lot of psychobabble in the form of DSM-style pseudo-diagnoses being spewed about in the form of character assassinations. Moreover, there was no shortage of unexpressed hostility to sort through. Warner cautiously arranged a formal meeting between McKenna and Cutter, where she would serve as a mediator and attempt to open the troubled and derailed lines of communication.

Warner learned that both engineers perceived their company as a place where "no emotions were allowed in the workplace." As the narrative of dysfunction unfolded under Warner's guidance, Cutter appeared to be somewhat disturbed when he learned that more than six years earlier he had gravely insulted McKenna. Cutter was apologetic and offered that "I had no intention of disrespecting your father. . . . I wanted to nail you and put you in your place . . . but not your father." In fact, Cutter maintained convincingly that he had had no knowledge of the death of McKenna's father at the time of the incident and could only provide a "belated apology."

McKenna appeared skeptical, confused, and at the same time strangely relieved. After a dense, awkward period of approximately fifteen minutes of silence and reflection (the atmosphere was so thick that it seemed as if an hour had passed) an emotionally laden dialogue unfolded. Some cuss words were exchanged, allegations flew about the room, and it grew increasingly uncomfortable. Following a period of verbal and emotional combat, McKenna finally responded in a reluctant but mildly favorable way to Cutter's apologies. After further prompting by Warner, McKenna in turn partially apologized. Cutter offered some words along the lines of "we probably should have brought this nastiness to a head six years ago." McKenna felt strongly that they had undermined the spirit and productivity of their division, and he seized the occasion to express this. "You and I have caused a little bit of pain and suffering around here . . . what do you think? It's been like we seeded the whole company with land mines. . . . If looks and feelings could kill . . . you could say we were mass murderers!"

They agreed that their conflict had turned into an ugly family and divisional feud. It was in fact a very dark chapter that affected all of SkyWaves Aerospace. Their coworkers had been dragged into the affair. In retrospect, the toxicity had progressed far beyond a mere one-on-one conflict. It had metastasized unchecked over a six-year period, rendering the division increasingly dysfunctional through the contamination of numerous colleagues.

DIVISIONAL HEALING PROCESS: CRITICAL ROLE OF HRM

Following the Cutter-McKenna dialogue, Warner proposed a divisional meeting to attempt to "bring our division into a healthier place and out of the dark ages." The HR director recognized that six years of anger, hostility, and silent scorn could not be erased by any sudden revelation or reconciliation between McKenna and Cutter. An insidious dispute had contaminated the division, and there was no reversing the costly devastation of transfers, turnover, and plunging productivity, creativity, and profits. Toxicity had taken root and spread deep within the psyche and culture of SkyWaves Aerospace.

Warner's proposal for a divisional meeting was initially rejected by both McKenna and Cutter, but after several mediations with Warner both parties eventually agreed, with reservations. They were influenced by their trust in the new HR director. The next step entailed bringing the engineering R&D leader, Julius Jefferson, into the picture. Jefferson was hesitant to accede to Warner's request that he participate in the "divisional healing process." Jefferson worried that the high number of transfers and the general turnstile experienced in his division would serve to dismantle the "good intentions" of this "emotional encounter group." Warner assured Jefferson that this was a worthy and potentially fruitful endeavor; there was a dire need to clear the air and address the deeply entrenched conflicts. Moreover, enhanced communication could provide some resolution and alternatives to the toxic behavior. Jefferson quietly agreed.

The breakthroughs in the McKenna-Cutter conflict were witnessed by the entire division of engineers, administrators, IT professionals, and staff. Curiously, the peacemaking between the two opened floodgates of confessionals. At least three-quarters of the division's members had experienced or participated in the conflict. More than a handful of engineers revealed that their involvement in the toxicity dated back to its genesis. A number of engineers, one IT professional, and several staff members individually acknowledged their role in spreading gossip, taking sides, and adding to the emotional turbulence. Warner explained to the division that the unexpressed emotional volatility between McKenna and Cutter had escalated and turned into an insidious and toxic contaminant affecting the whole company.

DISCUSSSION AND IMPLICATIONS

It was difficult to fathom that this six-year-old conflict was the eye of the storm, that a simple misunderstanding had escalated into companywide dysfunctional behavior. Difficulty between two engineers eventually encompassed forty-four engineers, the entire R&D division, and the whole global SkyWaves Aerospace network.

There was plenty of blame to go around; the fault was not simply with the two feuding engineers. Their battle was waged within a culture that worked hard at avoiding conflict. As expressed by McKenna, employees were expected to leave their emotions at the door. Was this written into formal company policy? Of course not. It was part of an informal organizational manifesto that was modeled and enforced by upper echelon leadership. Refusing to sufficiently recognize or incorporate emotional intelligence into their own leadership styles, Jefferson and Jones-Seaver had an emotionally negligent track record. When faced with people problems in the workplace they had a quick remedy. Send them off to the employee assistance program. SkyWaves Aerospace provided their feuding employees with eight EAP therapy sessions that were fully covered. The EAP was internal. But were McKenna and Cutter necessarily candidates for the EAP? Had other options been exhausted?

My reading of this predicament was that EAP was the local organizational dumping ground for human capital issues. If an engineer squirmed or barked, you promptly sent him off to the EAP. I believe that McKenna and Cutter would have responded quite well to an emotionally intelligent R&D chief or HR director who was willing to listen empathically and invest sufficient time to hear the intricacies of a volatile narrative. How do we remedy this? We must learn from our mistakes. As the external leadership coach and management consultant, I strongly recommended that Jefferson be provided "emotional intelligence training for leadership" and also be asked to participate in workplace negotiation and conflict resolution training programs offered by the Harvard University–based Project on Negotiation (PON).

Unfortunately, Jefferson and Jones-Seaver were not effectively addressing the dysfunction, but were rather in unwitting collusion with the conflict initiated by McKenna and Cutter. They did not have the skill or insight to serve as internal coaches. They lacked a working knowledge of the important role of leaders as toxin detectors and handlers (see Frost and Robinson 1999; Frost 2003) and did not adequately recognize or address the early warning signs of dysfunctional behavior. Eventually, when the toxicity level escalated and it was very obvious that organizational dysfunction was spreading, the remedy du jour was to send the pair off to the EAP. Unclear, however, is why the EAP regiments did not appear to have any notably positive impact on the Cutter-McKenna conflict. When the new HR director, Ms. Warner, inquired into the EAP findings, she was told only that the "records were sealed and constituted privileged communication." She was further informed by the EAP that since there was no diagnosis of danger to self (DTS) or danger to others (DTO) for either patient, any disclosure would be in violation of the Americans with Disabilities Act (ADA) as it specifically applies to psychological assessment and treatment. Moreover, because Cutter and McKenna did not request unusual or out-of-the-ordinary workplace accommodations, full confidentiality had to be enforced without any substantive or detailed briefing of upper management.

This leads to a specialized area of concern—the practice of psychological privilege and patient confidentiality in the diagnosis and treatment of workplace conflicts. In this case it initially appeared as if there may have been some symptoms suggesting a diagnosis. It is highly unlikely, however, that either McKenna or Cutter suffered from deeply rooted psychological disturbances warranting a formal diagnosis. As a clinician who regularly uses the DSM IV-TR in leadership coaching, psychotherapy, and management consulting, I was more concerned about the negligent leadership of Jefferson and the HR director, Jones-Seaver, than I was about any interpersonal or psychological issues pertaining to McKenna or Cutter. Although the engineers had failed themselves and each other, leadership had failed in a larger sense.

Colleagues and staff escalated the conflict by throwing around flip, uninformed, and mistaken psychological descriptions of the two engineers. The "pseudo-diagnoses" of McKenna and Cutter by unqualified lay colleagues with questionable or hostile agendas were highly destructive. Making a diagnosis according to the DSM IV-TR requires clinical experience and training. Although everyone has depressed days and exhibits narcissistic personality traits or tendencies at times, it is quite another matter to mislabel and stigmatize individuals in the workplace.

Mismanagement of dysfunctional behavior in the everyday workplace only serves to escalate its toxic effects. Low toxicity levels can rise, and mildly counterproductive behavior can morph into a dysfunctional team, division, and organization. The response to not-out-of-the-ordinary workplace problems was inadequate and helter-skelter; this mismanagement resulted in leadership collusion in the toxicity. I urge managers to systematically and strategically approach the inevitability of dysfunctional behavior (see Levinson 1976, 1981, 1987, 2002). Toxicity does not typically self-repair and cannot be dealt with impulsively via discretionary, reactive, and belated decision-making on the company floor. Dysfunctional behavior must be addressed in a timely and pro-active manner rather than reactively or as an afterthought (see Kellerman 2004; Lipman-Blumen 2005; Lubit 2004; Minuchin 1974). It requires strategic planning and anticipation. Clearly, SkyWaves Aerospace did not adequately prepare for or address dysfunctional organizational contingencies. What is required is a companywide cognizance and response to the threat of toxicity whereby dysfunctional behavior "becomes everybody's business." Companies may also want to factor in the presence and nurturing of toxin detectors and toxin handlers who unofficially emerge as internal coaches dealing with personal issues and conflicts in the workplace (Frost 2003).

SkyWaves Aerospace cultivated a "no emotions" policy that unofficially prohibited dialogue about personnel conflicts. The company avoided the emotional terrain and darker side of the human psyche and workplace behavior. The affective dimensions of behavior bordered on the taboo. This was a case in point of how an organization can breed its own toxins (see Lipman-Blumen 2005).

The engineers in question lacked adequate emotional intelligence and communication skills to resolve the issue on their own, and simple interpersonal differences led to costly transfers within the R&D division. Whatever the emotional and communication shortcomings of Cutter and McKenna might have been, the "no emotions" SkyWaves Aerospace policy obviously fueled the dysfunctional behavior. There was no venue available for constructively communicating emotional conflict and turbulence to third parties or toxin handlers until the appearance of the more effective HR director, Kathy Warner. Emotions are powerful, and they always find a channel for expression in the workplace—be it functional or dysfunctional (Buss 1999; Ekman and Davidson 1994; Goldman 1994, 2005; Lazarus 1991; Potter-Efron 1998; Tooby and Cosmides 1990). In the SkyWaves Aerospace workplace the emotional unintelligence of two engineers morphed into scathing nonverbal behavior, contagious negative attitudes, a lethal rumor mill, nasty psychobabble with the meanest of intentions, and an R&D turnstile. McKenna's and Cutter's negative emotions acted like strangling weeds in the organizational garden or a cancerous tumor in a human organism. The SkyWaves Aerospace case provides an indication of why there is a growing interest in the right-brain, relationship dimensions of leadership as depicted in corporate training programs emphasizing emotional and social intelligence (e.g., see Goleman 2006).

Toxic behavior at SkyWaves Aerospace shows why managers and HR need to be prepared to function as internal counselors, coaches, consultants, and facilitators for their employees (see Schaffer 2002, 2005; Whetten and Cameron 2007). In the SkyWaves consultation, the first HR director, Jones-Seaver, and the R&D division chief, Julius Jefferson, both failed to adequately function in these relationship capacities. Their deficit approach to conflict was one of avoidance and immediately passing problem employees along to the EAP. Upper management should consider that the failure of leaders to detect and work with personnel disturbances inadvertently increases the toxicity level and the necessity of contracting with EAP and outside coaching and consulting experts. Accordingly, I strongly recommend that organizations place their highest priority on encouraging emotional intelligence and toxin handler skills for management and leadership. Successful internal toxin detection, coaching, and counseling may prove adequate for many commonplace, low-toxicity conflicts.

COMMENTARY

The disciplinary lines have been blurred between management and psychology, as under the threat of dysfunctional behavior we must seek both short-range and deep-structure solutions. A failure to identify people problems is in itself a form of dysfunctional leadership. Managerial negligence undetected is a form of managerial malpractice and contributes to companywide toxicity.

As illustrated, complex webs of organizational dysfunction are frequently an outgrowth of mild unchecked toxicity in the workplace. In response, I submit that "everyday" organizational disturbances can be increasingly red-flagged by organizations as the responsibility of designated internal line and staff toxin detectors and handlers. As herein conceived, the toxin-handling function may be viewed as part of an expanded relationship and interpersonal function of managers and HR—rather than the exclusive province of toxin experts. Along these lines, companies can also choose to incorporate external experts to aid in the training and development of internal toxin-detection and -handling skills among supervisors, managers, and HR, culminating in a train-the-trainer agenda. In addition, organizations may want to consider strategies for enlisting large numbers of employees, or even the entire workforce, as toxin detectors. Echoing the total quality management (TQM) mantra that "quality is everybody's business," I suggest leadership consider that "dysfunctional behavior is everybody's business." Open-door, collaborative empowerment approaches to people problems are pivotal and may be combined with training in identifying and treating dysfunctional behavior to achieve continuous companywide improvement.

WILD P-53

Finally, as the company lies on the couch it learns that it is not exactly easy to distinguish where the nexus of dysfunctional behavior resides, or to accurately differentiate between milder and higher levels of toxicity, or to determine whether particular people problems are better handled internally or by external agents. Early internal detection is preventive and roughly approximates the timely X ray or MRI for identifying cancer cells before they metastasize. Cancer researchers have unveiled that there are preventive cancer detection and cancer fighting genes in the human system; they call these wild p-53s. Are there wild P-53 equivalents in our organizational systems, ready to identify and resolve destructive leadership, dysfunctional personality traits, and toxic company policies? Leadership and HR must address, initiate, and operationalize readiness and toxin safeguards throughout the organization. These efforts may entail the assistance of external consultants, especially when faced with systemic dysfunction, threats of terrorism and workplace violence, or instances where psychopathology is a possibility (Van Fleet and Van Fleet 2007).

As the company shifts its posture on the couch, different narratives and windows appear on the toxicity screen. It is an ongoing dialectic that engages internal and external agents and the best minds and practices available.

RECOMMENDATIONS AND INITIATIVES

I offer the following list of things managers can do to better prepare for the costly impact of undetected or mismanaged toxicity in the workplace.

1. Assume a pro-active, preventive approach to detecting and handling dysfunctional behavior; articulate those strategies companywide.

2. Remove the company from "the couch"; the organization must initiate and participate in innovative ways in solving its own internal toxicity problems.

3. In high-toxicity cases, the company's relationship with an external management consultant, leadership coach, or other expert is best conceived of as a partnership, not as a patient-doctor relationship.

4. Provide emotional intelligence (right-brain) training for leadership and employees, which is central to improving relationship management and developing toxin detection and handling skills.

5. Provide negotiation and conflict resolution training for upper management and HR leaders; see the Harvard University Project on Negotiation website for training schedules and options (www.pon.harvard.edu).

6. Develop organizational protocol for preventing, assessing, and treating toxic behaviors in the workplace; this may require the services of a management consultant with expertise in this area.

7. Designate managers or HR leaders who will function as toxin detectors and toxin handlers. Toxicity is everybody's business (just as "quality is everybody's business" in TQM); accordingly, companywide training in toxicity and counterproductive behavior is appropriate.

8. Review your organization's (and individual leaders') orientation toward workplace problems, especially as it pertains to personnel and relationship conflicts and toxin detection; I urge an open-door culture in order to minimize personal risk and a "no stigma" guarantee to participants.

9. Review your current grievance, mediation, arbitration, and/or ombudsperson policies to see whether they are compatible with and supportive of the other toxin-related initiatives raised on this list and in this chapter.

10. Provide basic DSM IV-TR training in psychological disturbances and pathology to managers and HR; this will enable your leaders to better discern between low-toxicity/common workplace problems and high-toxicity issues rooted in preexisting psychological or pathological problems.

11. Individual performance appraisals should be based in part on team building and relationship skills.

12. 360-degree feedback (see glossary) is recommended as a means for providing early detection of interpersonal problems and dysfunctional behavior.

NOTE

An earlier version of this chapter won the "best paper" award' at the Academy of Management (AOM) Annual Conference, Management Consulting Division, Philadelphia, August 2007. A case-study version of the AOM paper was published as "Leadership Negligence and Malpractice: Emotional Toxicity at SkyWaves Aerospace International" in Zerbe, Hartel, and Ashkanasy 2008.

3 Life-and-Death Leadership

The Case of Dr. Ivan Lorimer, Chief Cardiac Surgeon,
Eisenhower Heart Institute

> *If the surgeon's tone of voice was judged to sound dominant, the
> surgeon tended to be in the sued group. If the voice sounded less
> dominant and more concerned, the surgeon tended to be in the
> non-sued group. . . . Malpractice sounds like one of those infinitely
> complicated and multidimensional problems. But in the end it
> comes down to a matter of respect, and the simplest way that
> respect is communicated is through tone of voice, and the most
> corrosive tone of voice that a doctor can assume is a dominant
> tone.*
>
> **—M. Gladwell, *Blink***

Health care organizations are not strangers to dysfunctional behavior. Leadership researchers and consultants have found that professionals in the medical industry experience high rates of compassion fatigue or burnout, anxiety, interpersonal conflict, and in more extreme cases a long litany of psychological disorders. Stress levels are compounded among professionals working in emergency rooms, intensive care units, and surgery.

In this chapter I focus on a distressed and agitated chief surgeon and director of a renowned cardiology department at a world-class heart institute. Dr. Ivan Lorimer is in intense conflict with his surgical team, and the crisis peaks at the operating table during open-heart procedures. Faced with life-and-death responsibility, Lorimer and his team produce highly successful patient results but are increasingly threatened by a conflict-ridden relationship. The anger and emotional disarray among the team is gradually eroding their effectiveness. Several of the members are fearful that a surgical mistake will eventually be a consequence of the corroding teamwork. In addition, Eisenhower Heart Institute is going through a radical restructuring in management, shifting from an old-school hierarchical (theory X) organization to a more horizontally empowering (theory Y) model. The movement toward a collaborative approach to leadership draws on some of the best practices of total quality management (TQM) of the 1980s and 1990s and new millennium developments in Six Sigma (see glossary for the management terms used in this paragraph).

As part of this recent shift in power, members of the surgical team are questioning Dr. Lorimer and other superiors in a more open and visceral manner. Also, the restructuring is causing upheaval, flux, and an overriding unsettled atmosphere at Eisenhower Heart Institute. Medical professionals, hospital leadership, and the human resources managers are collectively embroiled and entangled in a difficult transition requiring that they have patience and believe that the new system will work. Throughout this time of accelerated change, the agitated state of affairs in cardiology has been of some concern to Eisenhower.

Numerous questions abound. Is the destructive behavior experienced by the surgical team primarily originating with the head of the cardiology department? Assuming there is some dysfunctional behavior on the part of Dr. Lorimer, is this attributable to a preexisting psychological condition separate and apart from Eisenhower's companywide restructuring? Are there traits or behaviors among members of the operating team that precipitate impatience, hostility, and intolerance during high-stress surgical procedures (see Brown 2000; Coombs and Fawzy 1986; Lachman 1983)? Do the reports of unrest and conflict stem from the flux, confusion, and upheaval caused by the sudden, massive organizational change at the hospital (see Pfifferling 1986)?

TOXIC LEADERSHIP AND ORGANIZATIONAL CHANGE

Dr. Ivan Lorimer is director of the department of cardiology at Eisenhower Heart Institute, which is located in a large East Coast city. Lorimer is renowned for his mitral and aortic valve surgery, conducting as many as four successful procedures per day. Dr. Lorimer's surgical teams of physicians, surgeons, RN's, and staff are directly under his leadership and authority. Lorimer holds monthly "surgical roundtables" to promote open and candid discussion and debate focusing on team building and any difficulties associated with cardiac surgeries performed over the previous month. The roundtable format was initiated by Dr. Lorimer in response to a participative management restructuring at Eisenhower Heart Institute.

Wide-scale organizational change at Eisenhower was precipitated by the CEO, Dr. Marshall Portello, in collaboration with members of his executive committee, who decided that it was time to "shift into the brave new world of horizontal management." Invigorated by the decision to put into practice a collaborative model, senior management reported that it "had struggled with some of the hospital leadership due to their old-school, hierarchical, type-A mentality." In an effort to flatten the pyramid, Eisenhower top brass called in the Durk & Borgus Consulting Group to develop an appropriate training and restructuring strategy. As a Durk & Borgus trainee enrolled in "Participative Management Training for Leaders," Dr. Lorimer was expected to unlearn his allegedly elitist, top-down approach to overseeing staff and colleagues. Lorimer and other Eisenhower leaders were asked to reinvent their relationship management skills in an effort to "horizontally lead" their departments and divisions.

Toxin Detection and Treatment

These "horizontal initiatives" were thought to be particularly appropriate and timely in Dr. Lorimer's case because Eisenhower's HR director, Cindy Morris-Julian, had recently received grievances concerning Lorimer's "outrageous surgical room behavior and uncivil demeanor." The grievances filed addressed Dr. Lorimer's "abusive and confrontational outbursts" during surgeries. Morris-Julian took the lead in response to reports of "a clear and present danger of surgical team conflicts." Rather than responding to the in-house allegations against Lorimer via (1) a formal conflict-resolution agenda and mediation conducted in HR, or (2) a referral to the hospital's employee assistance program (EAP), Morris-Julian served up managerial training as an alternative. She believed that the Durk & Borgus horizontal training initiative would provide Lorimer with "new-world skills" for resolving difficulties with his surgical team and help him develop more "squishy people skills."

Lorimer resisted participating in the training and expressed doubt that the contracted management consultants were sufficiently briefed in Eisenhower culture (see Schein 2005) or understood the value of what the surgeon affectionately referred to as his "medieval theory X" approach to leadership. The Durk & Borgus consultants struggled with Lorimer's publicly voiced challenges during training, in which he questioned "whether this participative leadership style is a one-size-fits-all, politically correct, liberal empowerment philosophy." Dr. Lorimer blurted out during a well-populated training session that the consultants were "illustrating outsider ignorance of the crisis issues facing surgeons." He erupted, "You guys are not in the real world!"

The training showdown was compounded by Dr. Lorimer's formal management and leadership background; he had recently completed an MBA program at a highly esteemed California university. Referring to his knowledge of organizational change, for example, Dr. Lorimer challenged the trainers by saying that "this 'A to Z' overnight restructuring is a dysfunctional approach to training. Organizations do not change their cultures over a few weekends." In response, the trainers assured Dr. Lorimer and the other hospital trainees that it was not intended to be a "shotgun restructuring of management." They acknowledged that it would take time to adjust to a more participative style of management and that some of the leaders, such as Dr. Lorimer, would have to "learn how to gradually relinquish and empower colleagues and staff." Lorimer appeared to fully comprehend their explanation but continued to intelligently debate the Durk & Borgus suppositions. He publicly warned his colleagues and trainees about the "impotent and floundering objectives of the training." He repeatedly warned his fellow trainees of future pitfalls: "Watch out! These high-priced consultants are going to turn us into a sick company! Mark my words, once they deliver a report and finish training they will be gone. No follow-up! Implementation gap! Sick company! We'll need massive corporate surgery. They'll have to put our entire hospital on the psychiatric couch!"

Lorimer never did make amends with the trainers, rejected many of the premises of the restructuring, and vigorously opposed the use of expert "outsiders" who were "aliens to the history, lineage, and intricacies of Eisenhower culture." Somehow Dr. Lorimer made it through the training regimen, but neither trainers nor trainees were happy campers. From the perspective of Eisenhower upper management and the Durk & Borgus consulting team, Dr. Lorimer was a "highly toxic force in the restructuring and training efforts."

When reports of Lorimer's verbal attacks reached the executive leadership, the CEO responded immediately. In an unexpected ad hoc meeting with the Eisenhower HR director, upper management, and two heads of the Durk & Borgus Consulting Group, CEO Dr. Marshall Portello expressed particular concern over the "antagonistic and disrespectful public behavior of Dr. Lorimer." Dr. Portello advised his associates "to keep a close eye on Dr. Lorimer. He has a world-class mitral valve factory going on over in Cardiology, but there is only so much crap that we can stand. I just want to make sure he doesn't derail the training regimen or wind up dragging us into civil courtrooms. I don't have a stomach for malpractice litigation or attorneys. Red-flag this Dr. Lorimer and let me know if he needs to be muzzled."

Surgical Roundtables

Fast-forward to the "surgical roundtables" led by Dr. Lorimer. Having reluc-tantly initiated them following his Durk & Borgus training, Lorimer attempted to promote "meaningful dialogue" and "politically correct collaborations" at these sessions. The roundtables were intended to provide a safe forum for build-ing relationships and sowing the seeds of camaraderie and collaboration. But in those sessions Lorimer unexpectedly found himself being criticized by col-leagues and subordinates for "inappropriate temper and elitist behavior" during two heart surgeries over the previous month. Dr. Lorimer countered that "this team meeting is hardly an appropriate venue for airing out our dirty and private laundry. Can't we agree that this is privileged communication and should be handled in a discreet manner? Why are you inflaming our colleagues?"

The agitated members of Dr. Lorimer's team ignored his plea and turned up the emotional intensity of the attack. Two junior cardiac surgeons and one RN publicly joined forces and painted a picture of a mad, irrational, and intoler-able surgeon who risked the highest standard of care with his "frightening out-bursts" at the operating table. Surgical nurse Sidney Gleesom shouted during an April roundtable meeting: "Dr. Lorimer, face it. You can't deal with the stress. You are suffering from some kind of anxiety disorder. You are suffering from panic attacks. Seek treatment and stop destroying your colleagues! The fish rots from the head down!" (See Mee 2002; Reinhold 1997; Rice 2000; Wicks 2006.)

In response, Dr. Lorimer seemed to become even more nervous and fraz-zled. He repeatedly interrupted the accusatory members of his surgical team. He jingled his keys and threatened to walk out of the room. He squirmed in his seat and paced the floor of the meeting room. At one point he took an incom-ing call on his cell phone and whispered in the corner of the room while the accusations continued. Eventually he grew silent in the face of the onslaught of criticism.

When it was his formal turn to speak, he finally uttered a few words in the name of "defending my honor" and his "impeccable credentials." Then he ex-ploded, "You are politically correct fools who value niceties and etiquette more than *life-and-death surgery*." Arguments ensued. Lorimer took the floor, and with a condescending voice reminiscent of a religious leader speaking to the wayward masses he delivered a memorable sermon:

> The patient is out for the count . . . unconscious. The anesthesiologist has done
> her job. I will yell in your ears at the top of my lungs if you are incompetent dur-
> ing the moments of an open-heart procedure. When I need you in a Code Blue

and state of maximum alert for my patient—it is here and now—not about fluff and feelings. It's about deliverance. Being 101 percent there for the surgeon and the patient. Is there any part of that that you don't get? Am I being unclear? Do I have to speak more slowly and articulate my syllables in order to come down the ladder toward your IQ? Are you with me? I am about performance. About surgery. About success. Not about sugar-coating some idiotic sensitivity chit-chat during the heat of the battle. If I was insensitive, so be it. I cannot respond coolly and calmly to incompetence at the surgical table! I won't allow you to kill my patients!

The roundtable participants were outraged at Lorimer's holier-than-thou speech, and tempers flared. The meeting took an increasingly negative turn and became quite mean-spirited. Negative ions and hostile thoughts ricocheted off the walls.

Human Resources Director Emerges as Mediator

Cindy Morris-Julian, the director of human resources, was quietly present in the back of the room during the entire drama. As the HR officer, it was her responsibility to serve as a coach and mentor for the surgical roundtables. In other words, Morris-Julian was there to oversee the "people process" and make sure that collaboration was the rule. Unfortunately, in this room full of highly trained professionals immersed in dysfunction, the chances were looking slim that the HR director would be able to productively oversee team building following the restructuring. Finally, Morris-Julian moved to intervene; skilled as an internal coach and consultant, she offered some positive remarks:

This is a sad day, Dr. Lorimer and good colleagues. I am awed by your nearly 100 percent success rate in surgery! How can we bicker and attack members of the Eisenhower family? Please, please, please . . . let's wake up on the right side of the bed. Dr. Lorimer, Dr. Purvis, Dr. Winston, and Nurses Gleesom and Malcolm constitute a brilliant team. We somehow made it through this conflict. Didn't we? The patients in question had successful surgeries. Please take a deep breath and congratulate each other. Our family is supportive! We *will* support each other!

Drawing on her "appreciative inquiry" training (see Whitney, Trosten-Bloom, and Goldman 2008b), Ms. Morris-Julian attempted to put a positive spin on a negative situation. She saw a toxic conflict unfolding that was in dire need of calm assessment and pointed intervention. In her role as internal coach (Whetten and Cameron 2007) and "toxin detector" (Frost 2003), her job was to be alert for dysfunctional behavior at her hospital. And as the "toxin handler" or internal counselor she provided therapeutic consults with employees.

But several months earlier, Morris-Julian had been slow to act on the allegations of destructive behavior by Dr. Lorimer and reports of dysfunctional surgical teams in cardiology. She had been extremely hesitant to call a private meeting with either Dr. Lorimer or the colleagues who had already filed formal grievances against him. She silently had debated whether this was a red flag for the employee assistance program, but decided to delay calling EAP and wait and see whether the intensive training accompanying the restructuring would soothe the wounds. But if anything, the toxicity had escalated, and it was past time to take a stance and challenge the growing conflict and hostility. It was high noon, and the time for avoidance behavior was over.

In boldly (if belatedly) speaking to the cardiology department audience of approximately fifty, Morris-Julian needed to be able to calm an emotionally turbulent room of professionals and also speak to the heart of the battle zone. Her voice was firm and seemed to derive from a deep reservoir of insight and understanding. Morris-Julian's words did manage to resonate in the room. Either she was a naturally gifted speaker, or she had some line into the ongoing pain and discomfort permeating the department. Following her brief and pointed words, the hostility appeared to subside. A few semi-apologies were voiced. Even Dr. Lorimer responded positively. He looked members of his surgical team directly in the eye and compassionately confronted those who had filed grievances against him: "Look. I am dealing with edge-of-the-cliff stress. *It's life and death.* Isn't it? So I go type-A on you! Excuse me! I'm a type-A personality and I let it rip on you! I freak out a bit when I see or even sniff anything slightly off center. I apologize for my hot head and outbursts. Our HR colleague is right. We have been successful." The divided, combative room of colleagues appeared to breathe a collective and cynical sigh of relief. Were the prospects for a healing dialogue emerging from the frenzy?

Internal Coach and Toxin Healer

Following the roundtable, the HR director and Dr. Lorimer went to a "chilling out and make nice" lunch. In a quiet corner of a nearby Japanese restaurant known for its ambiance, Morris-Julian started to melt the ice with the director of cardiology. She talked a little about her understanding of Dr. Lorimer's stressors and how the participative management restructuring was too much, too soon and contrary to the hospital's good-old-boy culture. Of significance was Morris-Julian's confession to Dr. Lorimer that there was in her mind much truth to his earlier attacks on the Eisenhower and Durk & Borgus agenda of rapid change and restructuring. She explained that in her view the company-wide change had turned into a "runaway train with many doctors, nurses, and orderlies unable to get on board ... and they were left at their stations ... so clueless." Dr. Lorimer was deeply appreciative of Morris-Julian's candor. He said that a surgeon had to at times be "absolutely in charge." He further offered that "democracy is not what it's cut out to be at the surgical table. You have to be a steward, a general, an autocrat at times." Morris-Julian agreed. Dr. Lorimer took it a step further when he whispered, "A leaderless surgical team is a frightening concept, and that's what some confused people on my team are attempting to orchestrate." Morris-Julian was a bit stunned. She did not respond.

Although Morris-Julian functioned well as an internal coach to Eisenhower employees, she was uncertain how to address the renowned surgeon, who was also her superior, regarding the high incidence of seriously counterproductive workplace behavior (Spector and Fox 2005). But she was able to draw on her positive leadership and negotiation training and attempted to assist Dr. Lorimer in reframing how he was relating to his colleagues:

> Look, it's like this. You are deal-focused, Doctor. The deal is your contract to do a successful surgery. But your team is also relationship-focused. They want some process, some supportive communication, a warm and assuring tone of voice. Your surgical team is asking for less yelling and reprimands. Regardless of who is to blame or how this all got started, they acknowledge that you are the man. You are the master surgeon and their immediate superior. But don't you need your team? How do we get to the people part of the equation?

Dr. Lorimer immediately grasped her point. Morris-Julian added:

> Lorimer, there have been three hefty grievances filed against you. That should be no surprise to you after the roundtable showdown. Will you play along and speak with the employee assistance people? Face the grievances. Deal with them immediately. Wipe the slate clean. If we try to avoid this and look the other way, we are guilty of kicking it up to the next level. And believe me, Dr. Portello does not want litigation! Once we clean this up formally, we can figure out how to get back into some camaraderie with your colleagues.

Morris-Julian's sincerity and honesty came through, and she was able to persuade Dr. Lorimer to set up an appointment with the Eisenhower employee assistance program. Having some background in clinical psychology and knowledge of DSM IV-TR assessments, Morris-Julian felt Lorimer displayed some signs of anxiety disorder. Although she was certain that the high stress level at Eisenhower Heart Institute contributed to the surgeon's outbursts, she doubted that other high-powered surgeons responded to the life-and-death surgical table with verbal attacks, condescension, and conflict.

The word from behind closed doors was that the EAP's assessment was "anger management issues" with no DSM IV-TR diagnosis of psychopathology. According to the EAP, Dr. Lorimer was a leader who was temporarily struggling to operate in a changing organization in a state of flux and upheaval. According to the EAP therapist, Dr. Lorimer's "exaggerated response" to workplace stressors were due to:

1. the abrupt restructuring of Eisenhower from a theory X traditional model to a highly decentralized theory Y, participative management model; and

2. the additional high stress levels of doing cardiac surgeries.

In addition, the EAP therapist found that Dr. Lorimer exhibited a somewhat typical type-A personality style by attempting to "force control" over colleagues and subordinates within this stressful environment and by blowing up in public and engaging in verbal confrontations due to extreme stress and frustration. The EAP therapist prescribed an "anger management training seminar" provided at another Eisenhower site. EAP further recommended that HR director Morris-Julian temporarily replace Dr. Lorimer in the roundtable discussions; she would occupy the role of facilitator at the monthly meetings, serving as a buffer and mediator for dialogue and diffusing conflicts before they escalated. The official word for public consumption was to be that Dr. Lorimer was going to cut back on his administrative and staff duties and concentrate on his surgery schedule. This would allow the doctor to enjoy official leave from the roundtable. The EAP visits remained privileged communication, and Dr. Lorimer was on the road to a more relationship-focused and supportive communication agenda. Even when he was fuming inside he called upon his newly acquired "anger management" skills to diffuse the situation through cognitive and emotional techniques. Ivan Lorimer became acutely aware that "being right was not good enough—it's how you respond." In addition to training and counseling, the surgeon maintained a monthly luncheon schedule with Morris-Julian that served as a therapeutic coaching outlet.

INTERPRETATION AND COMMENTARY

Was toxic leadership at the core of the ongoing surgical team conflicts at Eisenhower? As the director of cardiac surgery and head of the surgical team, Dr. Lorimer was assessed by the EAP as having anger management issues. The toxicity at the surgical table, however, in part predated the Eisenhower decision to restructure and invite the Durk & Borgus team in to lead the training. It had originated during surgeries, when Dr. Lorimer, fellow cardiac surgeons, and RNs needed to operate as a collaborative surgical team. During these highly stressful operations something had gone awry. The three surgical teams that had filed grievances all pointed to Dr. Lorimer as the cause. Allegedly Dr. Lorimer would turn angry, explosive, and intolerant when he felt that members of his team were not sufficiently responsive, attentive, or "on top of it."

Problematic, however, was the confused and belated handling of the conflict by the HR director. Although Morris-Julian exhibited many sterling qualities and eventually made progress with Dr. Lorimer, her approach had not been timely or sufficiently astute. First, when the red flag is raised, via grievances, there is no way to lower it. After missing her early cues, the HR director eventually took the right action. But initially she had passed the baton to the Durk & Borgus training team. Unfortunately, the plethora of variables faced in a complex organizational system breeds some confused thinking at times. Although explosive and intolerant behavior may sometimes be equated with extreme forms of autocratic theory X, type-A managers, this is a cliché and beside the point. It was a poor choice on the part of Morris-Julian to see the theory Y–style training as providing anything more than a restructuring agenda in which employees could learn skills for operating in a more collaborative workplace. Dr. Lorimer and his surgical team needed immediate assessment and intervention, not a reframing of the crisis as part and parcel of a massive managerial restructuring effort. Although the organizational change may have fueled the dysfunctional behavior and aggravated Dr. Lorimer's anger issues, it was at most a significant contributing factor.

Even more perplexing was the assumption that the three grievances and the threat of malpractice suits were Dr. Lorimer's doing. There was woefully little, if any, internal assessment of the doctors and nurses who filed the grievances. Perhaps one or more members of the surgical team were at the nexus of the dysfunctional behavior?

THE NINTH-INNING EXTERNAL CONSULTANT

As a late-arriving external consultant, I discovered in my initial needs assessment that although the parties who filed the grievances were granted a meeting with Morris-Julian in HR, this never resulted in a mediated negotiation with Dr. Lorimer or any timely attempts at conflict resolution through either HR or the EAP. Little effort had been made to examine the interpersonal or team origins of the toxicity.

In my capacity as the external consultant I reviewed all available HR and classified documentation surrounding the "Lorimer affair" and spent three solid weeks as a participant observer and action researcher. Part of this process included conducting extensive interviews with members of the cardiology division and the director of human resources. After the first week I focused specifically on members of Dr. Lorimer's surgical team. I gathered more evidence and observed that toxic interpersonal and team communication could not be separated from Dr. Lorimer's agitated and at times explosive responses during surgery and at the roundtable. Clearly the junior cardiac surgeons, Dr. Purvis and Dr. Winston, and Nurses Gleesom and Malcolm, were anything but innocent bystanders. Unknown to the HR director, Morris-Julian, was the fact that members of the surgical team failed to show appropriate respect for Dr. Lorimer's status as one of six mitral valve specialists in the world. Whether at cardiology roundtables, in pre-surgery preparation, or during procedures it was not unusual for Purvis, Winston, Gleesom, and Malcolm to direct caustic remarks, irreverent comments, and condescending language toward Dr. Lorimer. It became clear from observation at surgeries that the incessant stream of disrespectful behavior made it difficult for Dr. Lorimer to maintain rigorous standards for his assistants. This source of agitation was further compounded when Dr. Lorimer discovered piecemeal the substantive shortcomings of his staff when they were expected to "serve 24/7 on a mitral valve assembly line." Dr. Lorimer did not at first comprehend how inadequately trained they were in the new and groundbreaking minimal-incision procedure. In the words of Dr. Lorimer, "they had a decent grip on the theory and textbook dimensions of minimal incision, but were neophytes when it came to life-and-death procedures at the table. At times they were assets and at other times . . . gross liabilities." When, during the high demands of an open-heart surgery Dr. Lorimer lost patience with his team and lapsed into explosive and disturbing emotional displays in response to the pressures of their irreverence and incompetence, the junior surgeons and nurses in turn grew increasingly hostile. Dr. Lorimer repeatedly threatened to get rid of all of them and replace them with a staff "who had at least minimal training in minimal incision . . . and an inkling of manners and etiquette!" Suffice it to say that this vicious circle of toxic team behavior occurred at a most inopportune time.

Following my assessment of the cardiology division and the core members of Dr. Lorimer's surgical teams, I reported directly to the CEO, Dr. Marshall Portello. Although he had recently written a "memo of concern" addressing conflict and tension in Dr. Lorimer's division, Portello had been silently skeptical all along about the exclusive focus on Dr. Lorimer as the center of the storm. The CEO was somewhat relieved to learn that much of the destructive interaction was initiated by the other four members of the surgical team. Portello pledged that he and Morris-Julian would arrange for some "emotional intelligence" training for Purvis, Winston, Gleesom, and Malcolm and see whether they could be "mellowed out." In addition, I red-flagged my concern that the team lacked the appropriate training for Dr. Lorimer's specialized surgery. Dr. Portello pledged to remedy this deficiency. Meanwhile, Dr. Portello offered that "perhaps we are dealing with adult attention deficit/hyperactivity disorder," which could be "par for the course when you are dealing with a brilliant but frazzled world-class surgeon." I concurred, alluding to several symptoms along those lines. After a brief discussion of Dr. Lorimer's extraordinary training and qualifications, we agreed that Ivan Lorimer was not your average angry or discombobulated surgeon. We walked away from a second meeting convinced that Dr. Lorimer was a prime candidate for personal coaching.

Over a period of months I worked with Dr. Lorimer as his personal coach in both a clinical and a leadership capacity. Dr. Lorimer had not wanted to leave his studies in Paris with Dr. Artaud and his colleagues, and at Eisenhower he was unhappy among professionals who lacked his training, background, and temperament as a lifelong learner and perfectionist. In regular sessions over a period of ten months Dr. Lorimer made steady progress; he was on a prescription medication regimen and showed increasingly calm and balanced responses to the pressures of life-and-death surgery and the inadequacies and previously confrontational behavior of his staff.

But much remained to be done. My occasional briefings with Dr. Portello led him to suggest a long-term consultation and coaching assignment with Eisenhower Heart Institute. There was much at stake: internal grievances needed to be defused and potential malpractice suits addressed; and the hospital wanted to capitalize on the special valve procedure offered exclusively at Eisenhower. As the toxicity levels declined, talk surfaced about a "golden future emerging out of Eisenhower's darkest hours." The Eisenhower consultation and extended coaching assignment moved the organization and its leadership through toxicity into detoxification and a relatively normal state of operations. In time, the extraordinary potential of Dr. Lorimer's minimal-incision procedure became the heart and soul of a new surge toward superior leadership and organizational excellence. (Phase two of this story is told in Chapter 7.)

IN REVIEW

The toxicity that originated at the surgical table drove the acceleration of dysfunctional behavior in the cardiac surgery division. HR leadership was personable and well-meaning, but its management was sorely lacking. The toxicity level rose dramatically when Morris-Julian chose to remain a silent spectator through much of the heated public flogging of Dr. Lorimer at the roundtable meeting. Particularly troublesome were the public attacks on Dr. Lorimer by members of his surgical team. Their behavior suggests that Dr. Lorimer was not the sole instigator of the surgical table conflicts. Clearly there was an interpersonal and team problem. Public attacks breed loss of face and resentment, and they intensify toxicity and dysfunction in organizations. Retaliation typically follows. Much pain and suffering experienced by Dr. Lorimer could have been avoided. After personal attacks had reached a crescendo, Morris-Julian made a visionary and collaborative statement that went a long way toward opening a new dialogue and healing process. But it was just a little too late. Having completed Harvard University's executive training program and Project on Negotiation, the HR director could have been expected to function more effectively as a go-between, mediator, and conflict manager on the firing line. Critical to the world-class Harvard approach is the need to request a time-out ("go to the balcony") when tempers flare and personal attacks surface. Morris-Julian failed to provide a time-out or any other means for deescalating and reflecting when it was sorely needed. Despite the high level of the professionals involved, emotional unintelligence prevailed.

Faced with the threat of internal grievances and medical malpractice suits, CEO Marshall Portello contracted with Goldman and Associates Consultants in an effort to belatedly provide accurate assessment and intervention. An incremental, rapid-cycle consultation (see Schaffer 2002; Schaffer and Ashkenas 2005) revealed interpersonal, team, and systemwide sources of toxicity in the cardiology division requiring training of selected employees, consultations with the CEO, and leadership coaching with Dr. Lorimer. Breakthroughs pointed toward the prospect of a longer-term consultation.

IMPLICATIONS AND INTERVENTIONS

Eisenhower Heart Institute did not adequately prepare for or address toxic contingencies. It required a companywide cognizance and response to toxicity, whereby dysfunctional behavior becomes everybody's business. In addition to establishing an informal protocol, companies can also consider a more official and mandatory strategy for handling disturbances via designated toxin handlers (see Frost 2003).

The mismanagement of toxic behavior at Eisenhower Heart Institute points to the need for managers and HR to be prepared to function as internal counselors, coaches, consultants, and facilitators for their employees (see Schaffer 2002; Schaffer and Ashkenas 2005; Whetten and Cameron 2007). I urged upper management to consider that the failure of their leaders to detect and work with personnel disturbances in a timely fashion had increased the toxicity level and the necessity of contracting with the EAP and outside coaching and consulting experts. I strongly recommend that organizations place their highest priority on developing emotional intelligence and toxin handler skills for management and leadership. Internal toxin detection, coaching, and counseling may prove adequate for many commonplace, low-toxicity conflicts (see Frost 2003; Wicks 2002, 2006).

RECOMMENDATIONS AND INITIATIVES

The case of Dr. Lorimer and his colleagues at the Eisenhower Heart Institute provides the following lessons and opportunities for hospitals and medical settings in similar circumstances and for organizations experiencing potentially toxic behavior.

1. Expect surgeons and highly trained medical professionals to have been steeped in individualistic, hierarchical, theory X–style organizational behavior that is typically not readily compatible with a flattened, horizontal, theory Y, TQM/Six Sigma, and team-oriented workplace.

2. Do not impose sudden and abrupt restructurings and changes in management style or hierarchy on the workplace; overnight transitions precipitate high levels of stress, resistance, conflict, dysfunction, and toxicity.

3. Wide-scale organizational change in the form of radical restructuring (of a health care facility) requires time, training, and ample use of transition teams.

4. External consulting and coaching groups must not engage in "hit-and-run" assessment, training, and interventions of the type employed by the Durk & Borgus group in its work with Eisenhower Heart Institute. Training-the-trainer and on-site, longer-term implementation are required to offset implementation gaps and resistance to change.

5. Anticipate that dysfunctional behavior in the everyday workplace may not originate with a single leader; dysfunctional behavior is a symptom of troubled and conflict-ridden interpersonal and team relations.

6. Disruptive behavior in the form of angry or hostile outbursts needs to be carefully assessed to determine whether it represents ordinary levels of workplace conflict or a pattern of long-term pathology.

7. Expertise is required to determine whether an agitated and stressed surgeon at an operating table is expressing "anger management" issues or is suffering from an adjustment disorder as described in the DSM IV-TR. Accordingly, the organization enhances its capacity to detect and respond to dysfunctional behavior when a professional with DSM IV-TR training is readily available to assess disturbances in the workplace (see American Psychiatric Association 2000; Goldman 2005, 2006a, 2006b; Lowman 2002; Lubit 2004).

8. Open communication forums may prove to be undermining and dysfunctional; inappropriate and abrupt attempts to empower employees and flatten an organizational hierarchy can invite threatening public disturbances with far-reaching and toxic consequences.

9. The success of an organizational restructuring is greatly enhanced when professionals on board are included in the decision-making and are gradually trained and transitioned into a new system; exclusion of divisional heads, chief surgeons, and other high-ranking personnel is a recipe for conflict and failure.

10. The success of HR, management consultants, and leadership coaches during times of organizational dysfunction is highly contingent upon timely assessments and interventions; unnecessary delays can dramatically increase toxicity levels.

11. Private venues and safe harbors in an organization should be established as alternatives to publicly communicating hostility, anger, and attacks on the reputation and character of colleagues.

12. In a medical setting, ICU, ER, and operating tables are high-stress con-

texts in which professionals must perform, interact, and work together as a team; dysfunctional behavior is fueled by extremely high-stress events such as open-heart surgeries (e.g., see Bradford and Burke 2005a; Gunderson 2001; Scott and Hawk 1986; Seward 2000; Sotile and Sotile 2002; Wicks 2006). Relationship-building, role-playing, and other guided training agendas can be crafted to simulate pressure-cooker scenarios and provide dress rehearsals for life-and-death challenges.

13. In response to dysfunctional behavior in the workplace, more collaboration and team building surrounding dysfunctional behavior is needed between HR professionals, employee assistance program counselors, external management consultants, leadership coaches, and organizational therapists. Without coordination and cohesiveness, individual experts may function as individual entities, undermining and contradicting assessments and interventions of other professionals involved.

POSTSCRIPT

Subsequent investigation revealed that Dr. Lorimer had a history as a "hot-head" and "explosive genius" with a former medical facility. His behavior at that institute was reported as "not out of the ordinary for an elitist, holier-than-thou surgeon who was quite frustrated with the inadequate training of his cardiology colleagues, nurses, and staff." Moreover, as a middle-school student and teenager he had been diagnosed by a psychiatrist with attention-deficit/hyperactivity disorder, combined type (DMS IV-TR 314.01). Some questioned whether high-level organization stressors might have brought the cluster of ADD/ADHD behavioral patterns back into play. As Dr. Lorimer's leadership coach, confidant, and therapist, I was privy to this information and found that although his symptoms had been in partial remission for several decades, the possibility existed that the impatient and angry behaviors demonstrated in his youth could have been summoned back to the surface by the stressful environment at Eisenhower. My clinical assessment led me to diagnose four ADHD symptoms in Dr. Lorimer, indicating that he had "tendencies" but fell somewhat short of full-fledged adult diagnosis. His childhood diagnosis, however, remained protected and privileged information.

Whether or not an HR director, an EAP therapist, or an external consultant or coach views this antecedent behavioral pattern as the nexus of the dysfunctional surgical team and cardiology department at Eisenhower Heart Institute is a judgment call. What is certain, however, is that the interpersonal conflicts in cardiology and the toxic leadership behavior in question did partially predate the restructuring and organizational change at Eisenhower. With perfect hindsight, it is clear that the Eisenhower HR director was both negligent and avoidant in her response. Despite her good will and appreciative inquiry, she trivialized the dysfunctional behavior in cardiology when she initially "prescribed" management training for the allegedly toxic surgeon via the restructuring program conducted by the external training gurus. That was an inappropriate decision by Morris-Julian. At a later point the HR director responded in appropriate and even exceptional ways, but the toxicity had been fueled by her early negligence and misjudgments.

Edgar Schein eloquently directs leaders, coaches, and scholars toward the "wedding of anthropology and organizational therapy" (2005). In that vein, as a coach and organizational therapist at Eisenhower I unwittingly assumed the role of "visiting anthropologist" and became immersed in the life of the cardiology division. After several months I was no longer perceived as what the Eisenhower Institute's CEO had sarcastically described as "one of those slick, glib, hit-and-run consultants who stopped in momentarily to distribute questionnaires, generate quick data, print up a huge useless consulting report, and drop an invoice from outer space off with my secretary." During a several-month period Dr. Lorimer expressed that he "knew I was on the level." In other words, I was successfully operating as a business anthropologist who provided consultation and what Schein termed "organizational therapy" to members of this organization; I was eventually privy to information inaccessible to outsiders and not always available even to insiders and colleagues.

Without deep, personal, patient, and committed involvement by a leadership coach or consultant, it is extremely difficult to reach a differential diagnosis and gain access to the less obvious or invisible data from leaders and organizations. Building relationship skills and immersing the coach-consultant and clients in a complex and interconnected system is at the heart and soul of this enterprise. Anything less yields disconnected and fragmented interventions and assessments, which account for a low success rate with clients.

Unfortunately, too many corporate leaders have learned the hard way from costly failed consultancies. But they are not usually willing to disclose the details of their disappointments or embarrassments. I trust that this chapter points the way toward a healthier client-consultant relationship and furthers dialogue about ways to effect a positive transformation of destructive organizational behavior and toxic leadership.

NOTE

A shorter version of the Eisenhower Heart Institute case study appeared in the *Journal of Management Inquiry* as "Company on the Couch: Unveiling Toxic Behavior in Dysfunctional Organizations" (Goldman 2008b).

Post-Traumatic Leadership: Negative Emotional Contagion and the High-Toxicity Organization

Jarling-Weber TechSolutions Ltd.

> *Extrarational, intrapsychic forces can strongly influence*
> *organizational strategy, structure, decision making, leadership,*
> *and group functioning. These forces are not particularly easy to*
> *identify or to diagnose and are harder still to combat. But they are*
> *prevalent. They also constitute hazardous and persistent causes of*
> *dysfunction within all types of organization.*
> —**M. Kets de Vries and D. Miller,** *The Neurotic Organization*

Management consultants and leadership coaches are not immune from organizational culture and context. For better or worse, the external expert enters into corporate terrain that ranges from hospitable to explosive. In the organization of the foreseeable future, more outside consultants will be hired to help firms cope with high drama and crisis. Potentially traumatic events—from burnout, downsizings, and hostile takeovers to abusive behavior and workplace violence—occupy the dark side of the consulting and coaching continuum. Being prepared for worst-case scenarios is a priority: organizational experts must assess whether to enter into professional relationships with highly toxic leaders and organizations. If the decision is to proceed, what land mines and dangers are lurking? Hard data can be extremely difficult to come by when addressing dysfunctionality and toxicity. Anecdotal evidence and participant-observer field studies are the lifeblood of the consultant who is considering walking into toxic leadership and organizational venues of negative emotional contagion. By opening the doors of privileged communication and confidentiality, we can provide descriptions of and recommendations for dealing with the dark side.

At Jarling-Weber TechSolutions Ltd., employee burnout and the recent history of a toxic downsizing faced the external consultants and coaches. Their challenge was to negotiate and work their way developmentally from dysfunctional leadership, toxic culture, and systemic crisis toward positive leadership and organizational transformation. Can high organizational toxicity, extreme negative contagion, and leader resistance defy assessment and intervention? What if the client is deceptive and fails to disclose deviant motives, causing a pathological situation to unfold?

When the stakes are high and layoffs have shattered workers' lives, the role of the consultant who faces a fearful group of remaining employees can be very precarious. Does the client recognize the problem before it reaches epic, companywide proportions? Or will the consultant be called in as an afterthought, in a strategic ploy to offset a damaging EAP assessment, or a ninth-inning strategy to be employed toward questionable ends?

THE JARLING-WEBER SCENARIO

Jarling-Weber was in trouble. Massive layoffs had left many remaining employees traumatized, wondering who will be next? The trauma was not limited to those being let go, but extended to those who were still standing and part of the "rightsized" organization. Shell-shocked employees were faced with a harsh leader who just makes it worse. At Jarling-Weber TechSolutions Ltd., the white-collar toxic leader on duty was senior operations manager Max Lunger. Max had a way of rubbing it in, making you sweat, keeping you guessing, and taking your pain to the next level. A man of many words, he worked his employees over in an effort to persuade, manipulate, and humiliate them into taking on stressful overtime assignments. With a poorly handled downsizing agenda and an emotionally unintelligent manager who escalated the dysfunction, both upper management and employees looked for a better way to conduct business. Unable to reason with, communicate, or express their fears to Lunger, the toxicity escalated when employees saw that "all doors to management were closed."

Threats of grievances, litigation, and bad press required a response. When the employee assistance program faltered and management failed to generate internal coaching, Jarling-Weber realized that, whatever or whoever was behind the toxicity and dysfunctional behavior, it was linked to poor performance, turnover, and an overwhelmingly counterproductive workplace. After exhausting several internal options, Jarling-Weber decided it was time to look outside the company for an external agent of change. But once the management consultant came on board, the dysfunctional drama accelerated.

THE TRAUMA OF DOWNSIZING

Jarling-Weber TechSolutions Ltd. (JWTS) had been suffering from a post-downsizing turnover rate of approximately 38 percent for two years. Technicians, programmers, and R&D "fell like flies." A few programmers speaking in whispers in a corner of the company cafeteria said that the "sky-high turnover rate is the mark of a dysfunctional company." Other technicians and programmers, recognizing how tough it is to surge ahead in technology, said that Jarling-Weber was "only responding to marketplace realities." Eliot Orlack, a baby-boomer programmer who was the victim of one of the downsizings and right-sizings at JWTS, observed that "turnover in this industry is a fact of life. With technology changing every five minutes and companies outsourcing high-tech jobs to India, it's a brave new world. It's ugly for the guy who is a burnout or loses his gig."

In contrast, a younger generation X programmer who had survived a number of layoffs saw the turnover as a failure of the senior manager and the company. Hans Yerlichman thought Max Lunger and others in the upper tier of leadership should have anticipated the sudden and dramatic change in the industry. Yerlichman and a growing number of his colleagues were extremely concerned and stressed in the aftermath of the "corporate quakes." He was stunned by the coercive approach to cornering employees into overtime and found it impossible to have any job satisfaction or work-life balance under such extreme conditions.

Empowerment and teamwork used to be the rule at Jarling-Weber. But since the downsizing and soaring absenteeism, the teams were fragmented, and those who were left had to pick up the pieces. Human resources said the absentees or missing-in-action employees (MIAs) were people who remained employed but had been traumatized by the constant downsizings, rightsizings, layoffs, and firings. Unofficial "toxin detectors" throughout the workforce had sent up early smoke signals to HR (e.g., see Frost 2003). HR recognized the highly negative impact of company firings, but, unable to cope with the employee discontent, the director of HR, Miles Schaffer, shuffled the stressed, anxiety-ridden, and angry workforce into the company's employee assistance program (EAP), where they received diagnoses and brief treatment. Six sessions and out, with little time for serious change or recovery. Once the EAP option was exhausted, employees either returned to the workforce in an allegedly healthier state or they were referred out to external therapists, psychologists, and psychiatrists for more extensive treatment. Approximately 75 percent of the EAP patients followed through with more external therapy.

In response to the firings and layoffs, team solidarity and relationships were undermined throughout the company. The recovery, grieving, briefing, and training period for team members who had survived the downsizing became very time-consuming and counterproductive. Team and job assignments were in a state of flux. Once steadfast relationships eroded. Team members increasingly used the terms "shell-shocked" and "post-traumatic stress" to describe their emotional state (see glossary for definitions of terms in quotation marks). Rumor had it that employees who graduated from their EAP therapy sessions began using the DSM IV-TR terminology they learned from their therapists back in the workplace. It was not out of the ordinary for employees to refer to "post-traumatic stress disorder" in an effort to shock and unsettle their bosses and other selected targets. Foul-mouthed and misinformed amateur psychology became the norm on the shop floor.

Conflict in the workplace rose as job security declined. A few perplexed and seemingly caring Jarling-Weber middle managers huddled with the human resources department and with mixed emotions went along with HR's referrals to the company EAP. Belt-tightening measures were enforced by the company's internal restructuring guru, senior operations manager Max Lunger. In the personal lives of employees, family conflicts and divorces increased. A highly rated middle manager candidly told his superior that the "Jarling-Weber communal village has deteriorated into a viciously competitive environment where there are casualties all over the place." Also worth mentioning is the fact that in the post-downsizing era, workplace accidents, grievances, and openly hostile superior-subordinate conflict became more prevalent.

Despite the demoralization of escalating ranks of remaining employees and a slow but steady number of resignations, a significant percentage of the workforce still pledged allegiance to leadership. A small but vocal group of employees responded positively to what leadership termed "growing individual opportunity within a time of darkness" by taking on late-night and weekend overtime shifts for time-and-a-half pay. The receptive faction of the workforce collectively professed through a spokesperson that they "saw no reason for the soul searching, talk of change, or deviant acts of insubordination. We back Max Lunger to the ends of the earth and we know he's going to do us right. No question about it!"

DOWNSIZINGS ARE YOUR ONLY FRIEND, UNTIL THE END

Despite this limited pledge of employee support, the Jarling-Weber organizational culture was increasingly in turmoil. Clearly, turnover and insecurity wreak havoc. In response to incidents of counterproductive workplace behavior, leadership worked hard at presenting turnover in a "special light" to our "weaker and more vulnerable employees." Max Lunger simply portrayed the shock and flux as part of the company's mission of having to constantly "swim in whitewater." One maxim repeated by the leadership was that "turnover provides opportunities for the hungry and identifies and spews out the lazy." With the massive housecleanings and more MIA employees, there was a serious shortage of committed workers on the job. Max Lunger made it crystal clear that "the sky is the limit" when it came to how many shifts or hours employees could work. Lunger claimed, "Rightsizings can be right for you, my friends. The misfortune and weakness of some provides serious opportunity for the remaining, the alert, and the dedicated." He talked about the "limitless opportunity for earnings" at Jarling-Weber. Lunger mockingly boasted at monthly meetings with employees, "I yearn to find another $80,000 computer geek who wants to shoot for 150 grand." He repeated, "It's all about hard work, being determined and driven. I will fill the pockets of the 24/7 employee who rises to Jarling-Weber's needs! I celebrate you! We treat our positive deviants like royalty!"

THE JOYS OF OVERTIME: BLIND AMBITION AND BURNOUT

Max Lunger was quick to show off his prize employees at these gatherings. He brought them up to the stage and had divisional managers proclaim how much overtime pay they had earned over the past month. Lunger presented the overtime opportunities as an "incredible incentive." Lunger yelled, "All you need is blind ambition and to limit yourself to one or two hours sleep per night and I'll fill your pockets. I sometimes lose a few too many soldiers. Rise to the occasion and I'll put a smile on your tired faces."

These "mini-motivationals," as they were called at Jarling-Weber, typically drew ritualistic applause and cheers from the 1,500-plus audience of employees, managers, upper echelon leadership, HR, and staff.

Lunger attempted to make the rewards "too great to resist" and also believed that he was able to accurately size up the fear and motivational factors driving employees. On the one hand there was leadership's awareness of the quiet sense of fear surrounding the "who will be next?" drama in the company's era of rightsizings and layoffs. However, part of leadership's response was their repetitively positive spin and mantra surrounding the layoffs. But employees grew skeptical of the corporate spin doctors who proclaimed that layoffs provided more work hours, additional shifts, higher paychecks, and no detrimental consequences in the area of work-life balance. It was in Lunger's words a "temporary state of accelerated ambition, gold fever, and wildfire opportunity." But growing numbers of employees balked; it wasn't hard to notice that many colleagues were dragging their feet, falling asleep at their terminals, and losing all zest for life or job. "Depression," "post-traumatic stress," and "burnout" were the terms being tossed about. But Max Lunger seemed to relish ridiculing the "pop psychology mumbo-jumbo." He was quick to criticize employees in the hope of blocking their questions and challenges whenever possible (see Baron 1990).

The true believers and Lunger's enablers claimed that the massive layoffs were due to marketplace realities. Moreover, the offers for overtime were "Christmas presents" and "gifts of geese that lay golden eggs." Justin Standish, a chief engineer, stated at one of the meetings, "Don't believe the doomsday voices in this company. Lunger and Jarling-Weber are 'A-OK.' If the money is right, I'm all right." Sixty- and seventy-hour workweeks became commonplace. Lunger and Jarling-Weber claimed to pay their employees more than anyone else in Silicon Valley. Lunger and his associates strategically discouraged, penalized, and attempted to obliterate all "negative talk" of layoffs or burnout.

According to the company's president, Brian McCormick, the core of Lunger's job was twofold. First, he was to muzzle any public discussion of employee casualties. And second, he was to proselytize relentlessly on behalf of the emotionally resilient, workaholic overtimers. When the positive spin had worn a bit thin, Lunger continued the motivational agenda by lighting a fire under a few select employees. In his "Honor the Best" monthly calls he would publicly shower the alleged highest achievers with huge performance bonuses. Some of the more cynical employees in the audience likened the spectacle to a fundamentalist religious event, including the charismatic healing of true believers and the offering of gifts and funds in support of their deity. Growing numbers in the ranks perceived Max Lunger as the quintessential negative charismatic leader.

EMOTIONAL AND MENTAL DISTURBANCES

Despite the uprisings and growing ranks of stress-disordered employees, Jarling-Weber and Max Lunger portrayed to their constituencies that they had found a winning formula—one based on "serious rewards for serious work." The most driven employees among the workforce performed at a frenzied level. They were true believers in a quest for cold cash. But at what cost to the individual achievers? At what cost to the company? Organizational narratives depicted early-warning signs of absenteeism, failing health, relationship problems, divorce, and steadily increasing numbers of visits to the EAP with mental and emotional complaints. According to insider talk, the EAP had diagnosed employees with anger management issues, depression, post-traumatic stress, and anxiety disorders. Curious was the fact that only 5 to 7 percent of traumatized and stressed employees seen by the EAP had a record of mental or emotional disturbances in their past—before their employment at Jarling-Weber.

Initial EAP diagnoses of many of the employee/patients repeatedly pointed toward an organizational origin for the issues in question, specifically citing "negative emotional contagion" (see Basch and Fisher 2000; Frost and Robinson 1999; Henriques and Davidson 1997; McCraty and Atkinson 1995; Ozcelik and Maitlis 2001; Schaffer and Ashkenas 2005; Wood, Mathews, and Dalgleish 2001) and "toxic systems stressors" (see Babiak and Hare 2006; Kellerman 2004; Lipman-Blumen 2005; Whicker 1996) as affecting the mental and emotional health of individual employees. Behind the leadership curtain there was much "concern" about the insubordination of EAP counselors who "dared to fill employees' heads with drivel about the organization's guilt in making already crazy employees crazier." Word in the halls and behind closed doors at Jarling-Weber was that "the shrinks said we're working for a paranoid company!" In response, Lunger, with the backing of his CEO and the executive board, initiated discussions to "reverse the dreadful, poisonous effect of the EAP sabotage." In the midst of hostile brainstorming sessions one option surfaced repeatedly: hire on an external consultant who might reverse or "cast significant doubt" on the "malignant EAP drivel" and "help put the company back on track." In essence, top brass were 100 percent staying the course, and since the internal checks and balances were not working it was perhaps time to consider an external agent as a stabilizing force. After all, whatever one needed could be bought. Toxic leadership was in complete denial concerning any corporate diagnosis of pathology (see Bakan 2004).

BURNOUT: A "SOFT-TISSUE" PROBLEM?

At company "pep rallies" and "mini-motivationals" Lunger disclosed that he had been privy to the buzz of discontent, conflict, and grievances. Occasionally the "B" word (burnout) surfaced. Employees and management continued to whisper about an "epidemic of burnout" and "contagious negative emotions," and word had it that the EAP was fingering management for mishandling layoffs and scaring employees. Despite warnings from Lunger to the contrary, a few employees dared to speak out publicly about the productivity killers of burnout and post-traumatic stress. In response, Max Lunger vehemently maintained that burnout was a meaningless and politically correct term describing employees who were unmotivated, weak, and looking for excuses for their own failures. The senior manager assumed no personal or organizational responsibility for the employees' psychological health and rather was quick to offer that it was a "soft-tissue problem with no direct impact on bottom lines or productivity." Lunger stated, "I am well schooled in theory Y–style leadership and emotional intelligence, and I believe that our company truly supports our employees through troubled times." Lunger reminded employees that he wholeheartedly supported Jarling-Weber's "generous policy of assisting our hurting employees." In addition, Lunger alerted employees that there was always the option of vacation days for "getting your heads together." A solo employee called out to the senior manager during a meeting, "Sir, do you still support our employee assistance program? Shall those of us in fear of the next layoff stand in line and see them?" It was clear from the employee's sarcastic and mocking tone of voice he was attempting to publicly humiliate Lunger. Annoyed, Lunger left the meeting abruptly. Retaliation was in the air.

In response to subsequent public inquiries about what more Jarling-Weber could do to cushion the harsh post-traumatic impact of insecurity and fear on employees, senior operations manager Lunger replied, "Personal issues are not a result of organizational life. We are in the middle of a war for market share. The bubble has burst! There will always be casualties. What happened? The economy happened!"

COMPANY ON THE COUCH: ASSESSING JARLING-WEBER'S TOXICITY

Burnout and organizational dysfunction are a familiar correlation in need of additional probing. Although tough cost-containment decisions may be largely market driven, leadership must still assume responsibility for making the best decisions possible in a crisis-laden climate. In fact, if Jarling-Weber had reclined on the psychologist's couch as an organizational patient, the companywide diagnosis would have been post-traumatic stress disorder. In the course of practicing "insubordination," the EAP had left quite a few employee-patients with the understanding that DSM IV-TR diagnosis 309.81 applied first and foremost to the highly dysfunctional and toxic company as a whole (American Psychiatric Association, pp. 424–29; also see glossary).

At stake in the Jarling-Weber consultation was the role of downsizings, rightsizings, and layoffs in triggering additional negative contagion, burnout, and widespread toxicity. Shorthanded, leadership worked hard to motivate the remaining employees with high rates of overtime compensation. With the workforce seriously depleted, leadership attempted to turbocharge productivity by dangling cash benefits and other carrots in the faces of employees while simultaneously mocking and demeaning those who did not go for the bait or dared to speak of toxicity. Lunger's agenda was a bold, aggressive campaign built around denial and a destructive, deceitful reframing of corporate behavior; Jarling-Weber had become an Alice in Wonderland topsy-turvy world where "negative was positive" and whoever dared to speak the truth was an organizational infidel. Employees who rejected the overtime option were automatically labeled "lazy" and "lacking emotional intelligence and resilience." The subject of the EAP became particularly touchy. In breaking with the party line generated by the company's executives, the EAP version of the truth cast the seventh-floor therapists and coaches as "infidels" and "enemies" of Jarling-Weber.

It is worth noting that productivity did go up at first as a result of the much hyped overtime agenda—but at significant personal and company costs. A number of fearful and driven workers were initially motivated by rewards, but the additional work negatively affected their personal lives, morale, and health. It became evident that a sizable number of overtime workers were experiencing emotional exhaustion. Efficiency soon dropped, and many simple and routine tasks were botched. And the trend of dramatically declining productivity among overtimers was not limited to a few individuals; it applied to several hundred workers. Of utmost concern was the fact that the suffering extended to Jarling-Weber's overall performance: the company progressively declined and its stock suffered devastating setbacks on the New York Stock Exchange.

The burnout victims displayed exhaustion, cynicism, and frustration with the working conditions. A supply chain of burnout extended from the internal customers to the external customers, as several of Jarling-Weber's largest Fortune 500 accounts directly felt the emotional turbulence and the effects of burnout from the company's technicians, engineers, and sales and marketing personnel. Poor customer service placed Jarling-Weber accounts in jeopardy when they were no longer able to meet deadlines and provide the world-class level of quality and service the company was known for.

But Jarling-Weber Inc. and Max Lunger refused to acknowledge their position at the nexus of the stress and burnout plaguing the workforce. Instead, they steadfastly blamed the victims and defended the post-downsizing strategy. Victims were offered the "sandbox solution" of a brief vacation, or the stigma of visiting the seventh floor—the onsite EAP. Ironically and unexpectedly, the EAP option issued some hope to employees when they discovered that the counselors were "defiant" and "extreme individuals" who were "not about to be manhandled by Max Lunger and the board."

Max Lunger, when questioned by HR as a result of a grievance filed against him by a burnout victim, predictably replied that "burnout is an individual problem," not an organizational one. Lunger did not acknowledge its impact on bottom lines or productivity and rather viewed burnout as a soft-tissue problem to be handled by HR, EAP, or simply a vacation. Lunger turned to publicly ridiculing and demeaning the employee assistance program. After all, the EAP had dared to defy the upper echelon leadership. He offered the following when asked by an employee during a companywide meeting whether he thought the EAP was doing a good job of assisting employees with adjustment to the post-downsizing culture:

> Although I love those well-meaning therapists up on the seventh floor, we are not always on the same page. Bless them, but those silly little EAP people are a trifle confused and deceived by the cry-baby stories they heard from my lazy people. They're not the victims. I'm the victim. The executive board, President McCormick, and stakeholders are the victims! We'll have to replace that lame EAP group with some real counselors. How about another nifty downsizing, kids? I'd welcome exit interviews for the EAP bleeding hearts and eggheads. We don't need any more saboteurs or internal enemies around here. Or do we?

There was no solution in sight. Leadership was clueless about how to lead its employees through massive layoffs and firings. A few of them jumped at the bait to be bought out. Following the darkest hours at Jarling-Weber no charismatic, authentic, inspirational, or transformational leader emerged to reassure the remaining flock and put it back on track. What was left after the big gutting? A deep dark hole filled with fear, insecurity, anxiety, and trauma. Paranoia prevailed.

A DYSFUNCTIONAL CLIENT: IN SEARCH OF TREATMENT OR NOT?

Max Lunger and the executive board of Jarling-Weber were in a quandary and searched for a way out of their dilemma. They decided to hire an external management consultant. Given the increasingly dysfunctional organization and mounting crisis, top management agreed that an external agent would need to act swiftly. Somewhat familiar with management consultant firms, members of the board felt strongly that they did not want to hire a Fortune 500 consulting group inasmuch as they did not want to wait a year or two before receiving an impeccable and complex analysis in the form of a printed report. They were particularly wary of the old "Trojan horse" approach of consulting firms who brought in a slew of consultants and charged an enormous fee (see Schaffer 2002). They were more interested in hiring a results-oriented and hands-on individual consultant or small "mom-and-pop operation." They consulted MBA and Ph.D. programs in management and leadership, and an in-house Jarling-Weber researcher was assigned to comb through academic and practitioner journals in the hope of finding an appropriate management consultant and leadership coach.

Jarling-Weber decided on the Goldstone Group. When I accepted the call from Jarling-Weber I was thrust immediately into a highly complex culture of fear, instability, and self-congratulatory rationalizations. The firm took a good-old-boy approach to rigid theory X management. Its view of disgruntled employees was that they were lazy and would rob the company blind if they weren't micromanaged. Occasionally the management spoke in politically correct empowerment terminology, but I quickly realized that this was only for public display.

What the senior manager and the executive board were looking for was a reassessment of the bad rap they had received from their own employee assistance program. I was spoken at incessantly and did not have much opportunity to enter into a dialogue or anything remotely resembling a collaborative relationship with the client. Max Lunger and the board had everything figured out before my arrival. They told me that "a needs assessment was certainly not necessary since we already know what is dreadfully wrong with our company." They proceeded to inform me that their diagnosis was that the rebelling employees were a group of deviants who were "out to lunch." According to the client company:

> Despite the fact that remaining employees were lucky enough to make the cut and not be laid off, they are still acting like fearful children. The bad ones are not facing the challenge by working longer hours and refuse to help their company survive the onslaught of competition.

Upon further questioning I learned from President McCormick the nexus of the crisis as perceived by Jarling-Weber leadership. Many employees had been "contaminated" and "poisoned" by "liberal counselors in the EAP." The board informed me that the "EAP people told our employees that they were working for a sick company and it was understandable that employees would get a bit touched or mental in such an environment." They went on to explain that "this rubbish filled their brains and employees started to spread this psychobabble throughout the company." Top management was livid about the "poisons spread" and the allegedly destructive actions of the EAP (see Clair and Dufresne 2007). The perception of internal toxicity spread through the grapevine, in face-to-face accusations, in assertions between subordinates and superiors, and in grievances and pending litigation.

BEYOND DEMAGOGUERY: A DIFFERENTIAL DIAGNOSIS

Although I had been brought into their inner circle and informed of their self-diagnoses and allegations, I had no choice but to cordially inform top management that I required access to the major players in the organization in order to make my own needs assessment. This created quite a bit of friction. They could not understand how a "hired hand" would not accept the company's view of what was wrong and what needed fixing. In a heated exchange I prevailed to the extent that I was granted limited freedom to conduct a brief needs assessment. I gathered data via a series of interviews, an extended period of time as an on-site participant-observer, and through the recording and documentation of gradually unfolding employee and organizational narratives. It became increasingly apparent that EAP was largely correct in its assessment that the individual disturbances and pathologies experienced by employees were organizationally driven. My assessment also honed in on the high level of leadership toxicity centered in President McCormick and senior manager Max Lunger. Lunger, McCormick, and the Jarling-Weber organization exhibited symptoms and behaviors consistent with a dual diagnosis of a paranoid organization entangled in post-traumatic stress disorder. The fear, insulation, resistance to criticism, and expulsion of disbelievers via edicts and demagoguery all fueled and spread the post-traumatic behavior. Jarling-Weber possessed many of the symptoms of this paranoid dysfunctional type:

1. an emphasis on controlling behavior and thought process in the workplace;

2. constant scanning to identify threats to central authority;

3. suspicion, fear, or wariness of people both inside and outside the organization;

4. a centralized strategy focused on emergency, siege, and ongoing crisis;

5. long-term patterns of mistrust and suspiciousness of employees and the EAP;

6. a preoccupation with and state of readiness to counter perceived threats;

7. an acute and exaggerated concern with hidden motives and underlying agendas;

8. symptoms of an intense version of tunnel vision characterized by a laser focus yet paradoxically limited attention span;

9. an extremely left-brain approach to employees and colleagues: aloof, cold, and unemotional;

10. extensive negative emotional contagion and ongoing emotional unintelligence;

11. a pattern of long-term distortion of reality due to their suspiciousness; and

12. loss of capacity to generate options, new courses, or spontaneous action owing to their defensive attitudes (see Kets de Vries and Miller 1984; Lubit 2004).

It was the conscious, formal mission of McCormick, Lunger, and the executive board to diffuse this dysfunctional paranoia throughout the workforce—always anticipating the worst and manipulating behavior through fear, controls, and threats.

PENETRATING THE TOXIC NEXUS:
LEADERSHIP COACHING UNDER FIRE

The Jarling-Weber leadership held their breath waiting for the Goldstone Group's initial assessment and report. It was clearly threatening to them that I

insisted on (and was begrudgingly granted) a level of autonomy and indepen-
dence in my analysis to conduct what upper echelon leadership caustically referred to as "that differential diagnosis." It was barely acceptable for this highly
paranoid organization to relinquish control to an external agent. The consultation and coaching assignment was the exception to an extremely authoritarian agenda. True to form, top management hoped to be pleasantly surprised
but anticipated the worst from me. They were at least hoping for some professional ammunition to use against the EAP counselors. Some members of the
executive board were particularly concerned about "saving face" with a growing
number of former and present employees who perceived upper management as
condescending and dismissive concerning the EAP. It was a battle for positive
impression management, and I was the chosen professional and hired vehicle.

With my report approximately 75 percent completed and in need of several
more days of work before making a presentation before the senior manager,
the board, the CEO, and the president, I had an unexpected caller. Max Lunger
requested an "urgent meeting" with me. He assured me that it was "a critical
matter and involved privileged communication directly bearing on my pending consultant's report." I expressed my surprise that approximately a month
had passed since I had conducted personal coaching sessions with Lunger. Why
the emergency so late in the show? Lunger offered that "after you meet with me
there may be some revamping of your game plan." I scheduled the meeting for
early the next morning in my professional offices some nine miles' drive from
Jarling-Weber.

Max Lunger arrived precisely on time at 8:30 the next morning. He expressed relief that we were meeting at my consulting offices rather than on the
Jarling-Weber premises. Lunger immediately got down to business. He hoped
our conversation would remain privileged and off the record, separate and
apart from the in-progress consultation at Jarling-Weber. He further insisted
that our "sessions" would be paid for out of his pocket, in cash, off the record,
and "not entangled in any way, shape, or form with the larger and official consultation process." I immediately responded, "I am not sure that's possible. You
are in fact the senior operations manager of the company who has contracted
me. It's not that simple for me to change hats and treat you as an individual and
separate client." Backing off a bit, he qualified his request: "Look Doctor, I'm
in your hands and I'll go along with your judgment. Can we get started?" I had
the impression that Lunger was not quite sure how to express what was on his
mind. He was emotionally demonstrative. Before we proceeded I told him, "As I

see it, the most ethical and positive way to handle our time here is to keep it under the umbrella of the coaching and consulting contract with Jarling-Weber." Lunger begrudgingly agreed after some ten minutes of charming persuasion.

Although this was technically our third coaching session as part and parcel of the Jarling-Weber consultation, in another sense it was our first serious meeting as far as Lunger was concerned. We agreed that the meeting would fall under the category of "leadership coaching." But once we were ten minutes into the conversation it became increasingly clear that there was going to be a razor thin line between "leadership coaching" and "psychotherapy." This was going to be our first therapeutic session.

BEHIND THE CORPORATE MASK

Max Lunger's fearful bottom line was that he was "two people." He referred to the "public Max Lunger" and the "private guy with a conscience as deep as the Rio Grande." The public manager had been toeing the line after the downsizing, consistently being a "hard ass" and "cracking the whip like a dictator." To a certain degree the "conscious" Lunger recognized that he had been deeply engaged and entangled in what the nineteenth-century playwright Henrik Ibsen (in "Enemy of the People") had called "vital lies"; he had been telling himself "soothing mistruths" rather than allowing himself to "face the more disturbing realities beneath" (Goleman, Boyatzis, and McKee 2002, p. 130).

The public persona and vital lies were all part of Lunger's impression management. He confided:

> Maybe I have been lying to myself all along . . . telling myself that I do not want to consider that I have been an awful, unfeeling dictator. But the bottom line is that I have been motivated by the objective that I do not want my employees to perceive an inch of weakness in their senior manager. I have to maintain a tough-guy image and carry the torch for the president and the board.

Upon further questioning, however, Lunger revealed that he was "more than a little shell-shocked." He was concerned that "after putting down and mocking all of the double-talk about post-traumatic assessments that my employees came at me with that I will wind up being traumatized myself." In essence, the tremendous burden of overseeing employee operations after the downsizing had fallen on Lunger. Although he put on a brave face, it was in part a tough-guy facade. In Lunger's words:

I was eating my heart out over guys I've known for years who got axed. I know some of their wives and kids. I've socialized with them. Even worse, I've had to instill tremendous fear and dread in the remaining guys . . . the ones who survived the mass firing. Now the remaining guys were turning to me to save them. I've stuck it to them. Work till you drop or you're out.

I asked Lunger why the post-downsizing process had been so severe. Why were the remaining employees kept in utter fear and pushed to the limits? Why were they being driven to the brink of burnout? Lunger leaned in inches from me and whispered as if enemy agents might be eavesdropping on him:

President McCormick and three hard-nosed suits on the board keep leaning on me. I am their hatchet man. They basically lost all trust in HR. They are a joke. And they threw out half of our middle and upper managers in R&D. President McCormick sees HR as jellyfish who are in bed with EAP and condoning whatever they dish out. And the managers and supervisors still left are weak.

I questioned Lunger further about how he came to be the hatchet man. He was extremely forthright in his response:

I am the chosen one. It's not always senior manager work, but I have to come down the ladder and walk the shop floor. I have to do all the hits. I feel like a Sicilian in a stereotype Mafioso movie. I don't like it. It's killing me and it's destroying my personal life. I can hardly sleep, I can't stand looking at myself in the mirror, and I guess I've got a case of self-loathing. Until I climb out of this entrapment, I totally hate my life. But I can't hang it up. I put on a brave face every morning—like a woman puts on her makeup. I need the money . . . and it's good money. I've got three kids, a wife who I wish I'd never married, a mortgage, car payments, and you know that whole movie. . . . Am I trapped or what?

I did my best to keep Lunger talking. In response to questions addressing his stress and trauma levels, Lunger was explicit:

It's like I'm on a battlefield. This is a war zone. I'm not exactly soft or squishy, but when I have to blow my employees' dreams up in smoke, it's a creepy feeling. I feel dirty and disgusting. It's like I'm witnessing deaths and body parts being blown apart. It's like I'm throwing grenades and inflicting endless suffering. You tell George or Alfie or Stewart that he has to go packing and that we are letting him go . . . do you know the look on their faces? I've practically blown up a Scud missile in their pocket or opened fire at their breakfast table.

Lunger stands about 6 feet 3 inches tall and is long limbed, muscular, and formidable in appearance. And as his story unfolded it became evident that he did in fact have public and private personas. The public Lunger was what the manager called "the exterminator." But the private persona was hard-wired to his intuitive and emotional right-brain behavior. Although he was quite convincing as the shark in the workplace, he was also experiencing inner turmoil and much self-doubt. He questioned the morality and wisdom of his company's merciless approach to the downsizing. My informal initial diagnosis was that he clinically met the criteria for a diagnosis of post-traumatic stress disorder. Of particular interest was the fact that there appeared to be little in the way of a case history indicating that this was a longstanding problem for Lunger. Lunger said he had never experienced the extreme upheaval and anguish he was going through at Jarling-Weber. The trauma was a first-time event. All indicators pointed to the fact that the trauma experienced by Lunger was largely organizationally induced, not unlike the diagnoses EAP had made for a number of traumatized employees.

Curiously, Lunger also expressed some fear that negative emotions could lead to physical altercations, bullying, and other provocations "carrying the seeds of workplace violence." Lunger confided:

> It is unlike me to be almost getting into physical confrontations. As of late, the stress and anger levels have been through the roof. I've had a little bit of pushing and shoving with two employees and a nasty shouting match with one of the members of the board. I dared mention to a senior board member, Justin Karp, that maybe we were being a little too heavy-duty about how I was handling the mass firings. Karp blew up at me and accused me of going "mushy on him." It all worries me. It's not that I'm scared of a physical thing. I'd come out on top if it's head-to-head and toe-to-toe. But it's a mental and emotional thing. It's a nasty world to be living in when there is all this pain and anger about to spew out.

In the process of unloading details of ongoing workplace friction, bullying, and altercations Lunger surprisingly disclosed that

> there are at least two board members who are as disgusted about this whole thing as I am. They would love to turn this around. Somehow we want to call this a tragic accident or a death . . . we've been dying in this company . . . since the guns went off for the downsizing . . . bottom line . . . Doctor . . . can you see anyway we can climb out of this thing? Maybe I should say that I person-

ally, individually . . . want to climb out of this shit. But I don't want to leave the company. They're my family . . . a dysfunctional family . . . a sick family . . . but my family. I want to turn it around. I got two jelly fish members of the board with me. They probably don't have the guts to even whisper what's in their gut . . . but I'm hardly alone. . . . So to cut to the chase . . . I'm unsure, confused, and maybe I have to bail out and get the hell out of here quickly? Max Lunger and Jarling-Weber are not a match made in heaven!

Lunger proceeded with his verbal barrage:

Help calm me down. I know you do counseling psychology and psychotherapy. You're probably doing it now by letting me get everything off my conscience. Or are you coaching me? Just shrink my head. Be my shrink. . . . Anyway . . . get me a prescription. Chill me out. Talk me out of it. Whatever. Get me the hell out of shell shock. O.K? Don't tell me this is a private hell. Give me something. But I gotta say that I know the report you're doing for us, the consulting report, is going to be right between the eyes. Several of us already know what's going on and what's coming. But the important thing is how do I climb out of it? How do we climb out of it? I swear, this is a great company going through a bad time, and I'm a good guy going through a dreadful time. Do we save the company? Do I jump ship?"

The session was coming to a close. Max Lunger was struggling to retool and rekindle his ability to lead and was alternately exploring the option of an exit from his organization. Both Lunger and Jarling-Weber were caught in the jaws of a deeply disturbed, destructive, and poorly received upheaval. Lunger felt personal responsibility. The manager expressed a dire need to rise like a phoenix from the ashes of this nasty state of organizational trauma and burnout. He saw in himself the potential to be an authentic and transformational leader able to meet the call of a growing crisis. He was trying to find a way to be ultra-resilient, reclaim his self-efficacy, and restore hope and optimism for himself and the employees. Max Lunger was in the role of a post-traumatic leader, and his pain was inseparable from the pain of the organization. Would Lunger exit the company? Stay the course? Be sidelined by his trauma? Or rise to the occasion and be a leader in transforming and inspiring his organization to emerge from its dysfunctional state?

LEADER AND COMPANY AT A DANGEROUS FORK IN THE ROAD

A traumatized workforce and senior manager present a considerable challenge. In the case of Max Lunger, the senior manager had been both a formidable agent and a victim of a traumatic time following a severe downsizing. Lunger's closely guarded self-torment and uncertainty gradually enveloped him. Initially, he accepted his formal role within the company as the voice of management in intimidating and overworking employees since they were shorthanded. True to the centralized and extreme theory X style of management at Jarling-Weber, President McCormick and board members delegated the "eliminator" role to Lunger. It was expected that he would not in turn delegate this distasteful responsibility to lower-level managers or shop supervisors—it was to be his exclusive domain. If the employees didn't rise to the extremely pressing corporate need for overtimers, Jarling-Weber would be in dire straits and headed for possible extinction.

In the abstract, the fire-and-brimstone act was doable for Lunger. But when it came to dealing with colleagues, family men and women, and team members, the human element crept in and became increasingly difficult for Lunger to process psychologically. Despite his hard-nosed and surly demeanor, Lunger was not all left brain and without feeling. His posturing as the quintessential company hit man was being threatened by unconscious forces. Although he attempted to be as official and objective about his intimidator role as possible, the personal elements continued to seep in. Lunger did get squishy. He felt the pain of Jake Adams, Miles Cornfeld, Mickey Schultz, and his favorite supervisor, Glenn Ornstein. Lunger was unexpectedly and reluctantly finding himself in the role of toxin detector and handler (Frost 2003). The hurt, grave disappointment, and devastation of his friends and colleagues were emotionally contagious. As the highest-ranking leader in the company personally engaged in "working the workforce to the bone" during the post-downsizing, Lunger had no buffers between himself and the devastation. The "tough as nails" reputation that he had earned with President McCormick somehow no longer fit. In fact, Lunger appeared to be internalizing many of the threats to the well-being of his employees. He increasingly became a reluctant human sponge, unexpectedly soaking up toxins passed on by Jarling-Weber's many victims.

Mentally and emotionally there was much for Lunger to sort through. The immediate question, however, was how Lunger could move forward in his present predicament with Jarling-Weber. Lunger was searching for a way to make things right for his suffering subordinates while officially taking theory X marching orders and posturing as a demagogue on behalf of President McCormick and the executive board. For those employees already fired, the experience was a source of continuing negative contagion and deep apprehension. But Lunger and the others who remained employed were in an ongoing state of trauma. On the one hand, Lunger was seeking personal salvation and career answers through the leadership coach. On the other hand, Lunger was looking for possible interpretations and interventions aimed at reducing the high level of toxicity in the workplace and transforming it into something more palatable and positive. He was extremely sensitive to the fact that in the employees' eyes he was the toxic leader, the center of the dysfunctional and destructive storm that had engulfed their working lives. This was difficult for him to accept.

Ironically, the individual and companywide objectives were for better or worse intricately linked. As I saw it, the first stage of this coaching and consulting case immediately required some brief rapid-cycle therapy (see glossary) geared toward reducing Lunger's suffering and rendering him more functional. The second stage required that I move forward with the report and intervention proposal, belatedly tempered by Lunger's confessions.

Overall, Jarling-Weber presented a complex organizational culture at a dangerous fork in the road. Streamlining, rightsizing, and cost containment are part of corporate life in the big city, undesirable at times but occasionally necessary. The Jarling-Weber story encompassed many lives—many already traumatized, some profiting from the pain, and others looking for a way out. The psychological terrain became increasingly visible during my leadership coaching and psychotherapy sessions with Lunger. Field observation and on-site interviews with the president, board members, managers, and staff provided detailed descriptions of both public and private dimensions of individuals' lives during a time of significant organizational trauma.

An underlying theme that emerged was the Jarling-Weber approach to human resources. Max Lunger was given marching orders to expel employees in the most expeditious manner possible. No time was to be wasted, in order to prevent intellectual theft, retaliatory behavior, or anything other than packing and vacating. During a leadership coaching session Lunger revealed his duties in detail:

> Upper echelon dictated to me that highly trained professionals, unskilled staff, and colleagues who made their way to the elimination list were first and fore-

most widgets. They were human widgets who were expendable, and I was not to get involved in their professional or personal lives. It was strictly a hardball business and strategized as a slash-your-gut firing. You get the word that you're history. You're out. No dialogue. This is an edict, a decree, and a monologue. I was under explicit orders to say it to their face in old-school language. I was the hit man. I delivered the kiss of death. I delivered so many "you're fired" kisses that it seemed like I was delivering pizzas.

Lunger did not shy away from his intermediary status. Max confided that he was the man who carried out the sometimes clandestine wishes of superiors:

> Unfortunately, despite making way up there in the six figures I am only a delivery boy. The messenger to be despised. The messenger who delivered dreaded news without any semblance of feeling. At least that's the way it had to look on the outside—101 percent stoic and deadpan. Your job is history. If you have to die, please do it quietly. This is a civilized workplace with decorum. Pay no attention to this vicious, back-breaking message. Just smile and move out of your office. Good-bye. You're a widget.

It became apparent that Lunger was suffering from an acute stress disorder. After I carefully walked him through the diagnostic criteria and symptoms, he appeared to be somewhat relieved that his suffering had a name. DSM IV-TR diagnosis 308.3, acute stress disorder, gave Lunger a new purpose and a formidable mountain to climb (see American Psychiatric Association, pp. 471–72). His poor concentration, irritability, hypervigilance, motor restlessness, and impairment in social and workplace venues were all on target for the diagnosis. Of particular interest to both myself and Lunger was the fact that this DSM clinical diagnosis would render all of his coaching sessions completely privileged and confidential—not to be revealed to his superiors. Since Lunger was not a danger to himself (DTS) or a danger to others (DTO), his case warranted privileged status.

EXTREME CLIENT DEMAGOGUERY AND RESISTANCE

The "bullet to the brain"-style downsizing (Lunger's words) did not provide the clean kill intended by top brass. The flood of grievances, pending litigation, and some very bad press plagued the president and board members. Until I heard Lunger's privileged confessions I had received no concrete description of the extent of the toxicity. The negative contagion was longstanding, deeply rooted in the organization, and extremely resistant to diagnosis or intervention. A collectively paranoid type A personality operated at the top of the organization. The solidarity in pathology was fierce and seemingly immovable. In the demagogic collective mind of Jarling-Weber's leadership they were obviously 100 percent correct in their decision-making, and whether it was Lunger or an external management consultant, we were hired hands on short tethers and expected to follow orders explicitly. The consultant was to tidy up after the president, the senior manager of operations, and the executive board and exhibit superhuman "impression management" skills in the course of stopping the internal corporate bleeding and conducting damage control with the media. There was one major problem, however. The old game was no longer working. Even the executive board housed two unidentified members who were potential defectors. Would they step forward? The house of cards was about to come down. Lawsuits were already scheduled on the civil dockets. The senior manager of operations and top-tier leadership were emotionally drained and paying the price for playing the toxic game. The organizational culture had been traumatized. As disclosed by Lunger, the post-traumatic state of individual employees was not a fiction. Clearly there was much truth in the EAP diagnoses that the upper echelon was so intent on silencing.

Unfortunately, the assessment triggered by the senior manager's unexpected confessions revealed that a very serious housecleaning was in order, extending down to the deep structure and foundations of the Jarling-Weber culture, including values, strategy, HR, and operations. Once I had an adequate opportunity to sift through the data collected on-site and had fully digested the "wild-card sessions" with the manager, it became clear that Jarling-Weber was using its external expert (me) to achieve the peripheral and unethical goal of invalidating the EAP. It was the brainchild of President McCormick that by degrading and trivializing the EAP's diagnosis of post-traumatic stress among numerous employees he could somehow make the truth go away. As the external consultant, I was expected to invalidate Jarling-Weber's EAP and thereby validate the upper echelon leadership's demagoguery. Behind closed doors I was ordered to "destroy and mock the EAP's credibility, overturn any notion that there was a companywide pathology, and thoroughly and clinically sterilize the Jarling-Weber brand name." In other words, the employees who were downsized were supposed to be portrayed as nothing more than angry individuals who wanted to retaliate against Jarling-Weber.

Of special concern in my assessment of the company were the irrational, explosive, and paranoid edicts and demands of President McCormick, who mandated that "the entire EAP be discredited, publicly humiliated, and professionally reprimanded for their false and malicious diagnoses of individual employees and the entire organization." In fact, EAP was substantively correct in its diagnoses and Jarling-Weber's upper echelon leadership was in denial.

From start to finish, Jarling-Weber's reasoning was tragically flawed. First, they got more than they bargained for when they entrusted Max Lunger to eliminate employees as if they were disposable widgets. Although he appeared to perfectly perform the demagogic role mandated by the president and the majority of the executive board—his conscience got the better of him. He wanted to save the farm and the family. And next, they chose the wrong consulting group when they hired me to validate their actions.

VENDETTA: PREAMBLE TO THE CONSULTANT'S REPORT

I debated whether to make a face-to-face presentation of my consultant's report or to deliver the document as an e-mail attachment. Max Lunger forewarned me to avoid the showdown and certain catastrophe that would result from a "sit-down" with President McCormick and his board. I decided to pose the question to Dr. McCormick, and I was more than a bit surprised by his surly response. McCormick appeared agitated by the very mention of the report and abruptly stated that a printed document and e-mail attachment would be his preference—followed by a face-to-face consult. McCormick seized the moment and spoke in a scolding and memorable voice:

> Look, Mr. Goldstone, just make sure that there won't be any loose ends with the report or any aspect of this consultation. I expect the e-mailed report *and* the hard copy in one week. Keep in mind that I don't have any intention of rapping, discussing, debating, conversing, or dialoging with you in any way, shape, or form before receiving the report. Please don't ask me to do your job! You're the expert, and Jarling-Weber is digging into our pockets to pay for your expertise. I am only interested in you delivering a complete package to me. Once again, *show up with a complete package without any loose ends.* You and your colleagues are the experts. And as we have personally discussed, I expect a full-throttle thrashing of that embarrassing EAP at the core of the report.

As soon as his tirade was complete, he motioned me to exit his office suite with a gesture of his head and chin. Though his edict was clear, it is difficult to fully convey the extent of the hostility embodied in his tone of voice, facial expression, and the overall subtext.

If there had been any doubt or thought of wiggle room in dealing with Dr. McCormick, this was eradicated by his most recent and troubled behavior. It was apparent that the nexus of the paranoid organization and the post-traumatic leadership and companywide burnout was located in Dr. McCormick's executive suite (and to a certain degree it also emanated from several board members). But the inconvenient truth was that Dr. McCormick himself was 101 percent off-limits during my assessment work. He condescendingly refused to consent to an interview. Dr. McCormick's demagoguery extended from the organization into the consultation.

D-DAY: CONSULTANT'S REPORT TO JARLING-WEBER

The report clearly articulated much of what Dr. McCormick and some of the board members did not want to hear. The layoffs had been traumatic to the remaining members of the workforce. I explained that their anxiety had been compounded by the company's destructive approach of soliciting overtime hours and a variety of leader-generated coercive behaviors. This composite culminated in companywide burnout and EAP reports of individual psychopathologies.

The fourteen-point diagnosis or assessment portion of the report was followed by a "recommended interventions" section. Foremost in my view was need for a leadership transition from demagoguery and intimidation into a relationship-oriented leadership strategy committed to building psychological capital and resilience (see Luthans, Youssef, and Avolio 2007a, 2007b). A few of the interventions recommended included:

1. acknowledging burnout and widespread cases of post-traumatic stress throughout the workforce;

2. more dialogue and the reinstatement of therapists and coaches within the employee assistance program;

3. cautious, emotionally, and culturally intelligent use of 360-degree feedback (see glossary);

4. empowerment strategies for the remaining employees;

5. bimonthly meetings of relationship-building teams attended by supervisors, managers, and upper-tier leadership;

6. the creation of at least five alternative options to the heavy-handed persuasion and manipulation of remaining employees to work excessive overtime hours; and

7. a strong recommendation to include a rightsizing dimension to the downsizing, providing a few strategic new hires to offset some of the heavy workforce losses.

LEADERS RESPOND TO THE REPORT

Dr. McCormick was extremely displeased with the consultant's report. His edicts and threats did not produce the results he had mandated. Several board members fully backed the president by unanimously condemning the consultant and the report, rendering it "null and void." Max Lunger remained quiet during the meeting of upper management and deferred to his colleagues. The immediate actions taken by McCormick and the board included the termination of the consulting contract with Goldstone. McCormick then undertook his own housecleaning plan, marked by the elimination of the longstanding employee assistance program and the securing of another EAP group known for online coaching and therapy. Within three weeks of the termination of Goldstone Consultants, Max Lunger handed in his formal resignation, despite threats of being "terminally and globally blacklisted" by President McCormick.

THE DEMAGOGUE CLIENT ORGANIZATION: CASTING THE CONSULTANT AS A PAWN IN THEIR GAME

Toxic managers and dysfunctional organizations may profess to be looking for solutions and treatment, but there is probably more going on than is initially visible (see Kets de Vries 1984, 1995). Some organizations reiterate and project their deeply rooted individual and organizational pathology through the manner in which they deal with external consultants (e.g., see Kilberg, 2000; Levinson, 1972). Jarling-Weber used the consultant as a pawn in their game. In this consultation it was clear to me that the only way to move toward positive change was to work with the senior manager and top leadership toward an acknowledgment of the negative emotional contagion and toxicity producing burnout and post-traumatic stress (see Clair and Dufresne 2007; James and Wooten 2005). Surprisingly, the senior manager who had been forced into the role of enforcer disclosed his own turmoil and agony over occupying the role of demagogue and searched for a way out through leadership coaching. It became increasingly apparent that the primary source of the fire and brimstone and the dark force in the Jarling-Weber downsizing and burnout was the president, Dr. McCormick. McCormick, unlike Lunger, was steadfast in his commitment to extreme theory X and the vertical deployment of his commands. Throughout the consultation President McCormick personified the paranoid state and post-traumatic stress enveloping the organization. McCormick was guarded and suspicious of any and all assessment and investigation by the consultants. Why was I prying? Why didn't I just accept his word and proceed with a humiliation of the EAP and a disqualification of all of their diagnoses? In one interview session McCormick exploded at me and said:

> Why are you asking me this crap? I'm not the source of the problems around here. There's a lot of sickness, Doctor. Since you want to use the stethoscope, go out there and find the freaking virus that started this all! It's in the EAP. You don't have to look too hard or too far. EAP is poison. We've been infected!

POSTSCRIPT

Some two years after I exited this short-lived consultation, the company filed for bankruptcy. Sometimes organizational toxicity runs so deep that a company must kill itself off. No management consultant, executive coach, or organizational therapist can save it. Social scientists, consultants, and even so-called holy men have their limits.

On a brighter note, Max Lunger gradually emerged from his acute stress disorder to reinvent himself as an instructor at a state university. I continued my dialogue with Lunger, and he now works with an executive consulting group as a trainer and consultant. Max Lunger offers clients some extraordinary insights into negative emotional contagion, toxic leadership, and client resistance. Moreover, he is able to provide an inside track to others on the road to hope, optimism, self-efficacy, and resilience. In the end, he did rise like a phoenix from the ashes of Jarling-Weber.

5 Reinventing the Toxic Leader: Negotiating Through Upper Echelon Dissonance and Resistance

EuroText International

> *EuroText's longstanding and admired senior manager, David Gravestone, had been mired in a messy public divorce and child custody case. The usually steadfast and grounded leader appeared to lose his firm old-school grip on EuroText's operations. Normally a consummate professional, Gravestone was not himself. He became increasingly moody and argumentative, and he engaged in bullying behavior with subordinates; his personal makeover attracted much attention. Whispers of "narcissist" . . . floated through the hallways.*

It comes as no surprise that calamity and crisis can spur an organization to take action. Assessments have to be made and interventions planned. In this chapter I examine the role of the management consultant and leadership coach as external expert, partner, and advocate on behalf of a client organization that has been unable to cope affectively (or effectively) with toxic leadership and companywide dissonance. Although often conceived of as a rarefied and private affair, the client-consultant relationship warrants closer examination. In this chapter I describe in detail the behind-the-scenes conflict and negotiations in consultations and explain why the success of a consultation is contingent on a healthy client-consultant collaboration. I describe the phenomenology of a single consultation's evolution over time, focusing specifically on the difficulties in achieving a transition from a consultant-centered to a client-centered model.

AN ORGANIZATIONAL WAKE-UP CALL

When things go wrong, leaders respond. Organizations seek explanations for a counterproductive workplace. They call on consultants to assess what has triggered employee complaints and grievances, absenteeism, interpersonal conflict, clashes with leadership, insubordination, and faltering productivity. They are especially concerned about reports of toxic leadership behavior. In the case of EuroText, an information technology company based in Brussels, Belgium, the top tier understood that they were suffering from numerous people problems but couldn't quite get at the root causes. Caught in a quagmire of conflict and plunging morale, the corporation initially struggled to resolve its problems internally. After companywide efforts led by management and human resources failed to yield insight or solutions, the leadership was prompted to seek out an external expert.

CHOOSING A COACH AND CONSULTANT

The choice of a coaching and consulting group was a significant decision. Should EuroText hire experts who make house calls to sick organizations? Such a consultant-as-doctor would be expected to diagnose, treat, and nurse the organization-as-patient back to health (see Gallessich 1982; Kets de Vries 2007). Or should the ailing EuroText perceive itself as a player and partner in the consultation and operate from a client-centered perspective? Following deliberation among the top managers, the HR director, the president and CEO, and executive board members, the consensus was that EuroText preferred a vertical, doctor-patient relationship that would diagnose the organizational illness and provide medication in the form of interventions. At stake was the company's goal of "uplifting the faltering EuroText giant and silencing a workforce caught in a downward spiral." The upper echelon was "upset with workers who dared balk at the long-term leadership of brilliant senior manager David Gravestone." Through a consultation, the firm's leaders hoped to dispel the rumors that EuroText's personnel problems were somehow linked to the allegedly toxic behavior of Gravestone.

EuroText was convinced that by landing the right leadership coach and consulting group they would be able to pave their way back to positive organizational behavior (see Farson 1997; Nelson and Cooper 2007). CEO Colin Cavendish believed that "leadership coaching could assist Gravestone in making it through a trying time marked by an unappreciative and fickle workforce." In addition, there was a consensus among Cavendish, Gravestone, and executive board members that "an assessment and positive intervention by a highly skilled leadership coach and management consulting group would be instrumental in turning around the fortunes of EuroText, a once proud and industry leading IT innovator in Western Europe and around the world."

PRIVILEGED CONSULTATIONS BETWEEN CLIENT AND CONSULTANT

In the course of searching for the appropriate consulting group, EuroText's president and CEO were struck by the shroud of mystery surrounding the client-consultant relationship. As novices in the process, the selection committee wondered why there were so few candid reports on the intricacies of coaching and consulting with corporate clients. When the EuroText leaders asked potential consultants for specifics about their previous work, they received responses such as, "this is classified information, and it is as privileged as the exchanges between psychotherapist and patient or priest and confessor." But without any specifics or a fundamental understanding of the consulting process, EuroText was uneasy about entering into the intangible and difficult-to-measure zone of external experts. The EuroText team designated to choose a consulting and coaching group wanted to know:

- On what basis do you choose a consulting and coaching group?
- What should the corporate client expect from a consultancy or leadership coaching?
- What kind of relationship develops between consultants, coaches, and clients? Vertical? Horizontal? A hybrid?
- What are some of the best- and worst-case consulting and coaching scenarios?
- Can we benchmark successful or extraordinary coaching and consultancies?

In their research, EuroText found that there was no shortage of theorists and practitioners with opinions about improving coaching and consultant communication with clients and incorporating clients more into consultations (see Block and Markowitz 2000; Lowman 2002; Schein 1969, 1988). But they could find few descriptions and interpretations of the actual play-by-play, the interpersonal drama, and the relationships that shape these crucial business transactions. The EuroText search team thought there was a need for consultants and coaches to find ways to divulge the micro-organizational behavior and interpersonal dimensions of this sometimes messy and fully human terrain (see Goldman 2007; Zaleznik 2007). This largely invisible world of consultations takes place behind the curtains of client privilege and confidentiality. But EuroText wanted to understand the wide spectrum of consultant-client interactions: strategies and agendas; restraints; resistance; internal politics;

negotiations; conflicts; and developmental issues (see Engellau 2007; Kipping and Engwall 2002; Schaffer 2002). Despite all the business and media attention surrounding professional coaches and consulting groups, little is known about the dynamic "people side" of the work and the relationship between external experts and companies (Bradford and Burke 2005b). Would EuroText have to learn the hard way?

EUROTEXT CONTRACTS WITH DT&G CONSULTING

After conducting its research, the EuroText search team decided on Davis, Travis & Grambling Coaching and Consulting Group (DT&G). DT&G maintains offices in Cambridge-Boston, Massachusetts, and London. Attracted to the many corporate and leadership successes of the DT&G group with both North American and European clients, EuroText chose a consultant more inclined toward a client-centered empowerment approach than toward the hierarchical medical model preferred by the company's leadership. One important consideration was DT&G's location in both Western Europe and the United States, where EuroText also operated.

Management consultants and leadership coaches recognize that organizations seldom call during the early days of workplace conflict or toxic leadership (see Farson 1997). Likewise, EuroText sought an external consultant only after the organizational bleeding had reached a crisis state. A multitude of workplace grievances had been compiled, with litigation pending. Stockholders were exerting public pressure on the leadership. Several relocations of key mid-level managers to U.S.-based EuroText plants in Colorado and California continued to be points of contention among Brussels loyalists. Grievances addressed acts of workplace sabotage, transfers of dissident managers, and toxic treatment by the company's leaders. Stories about the toxicity of long-term senior manager David Gravestone abounded. Following a period of agitation and numerous reports of leader toxicity, Gravestone largely withdrew from the workplace, becoming an absentee leader. EuroText publicly defended Gravestone, but his superiors were privately dumbfounded. Hoping to reverse Gravestone's destructive behavior, EuroText expedited the consultancy search and came up with a highly recommended team, albeit one that preferred to work more collaboratively than hierarchically.

From its first day on the EuroText campus, the Davis, Travis & Grambling Group were inundated with the upper echelon leadership's version of its symptoms. They had already determined the cause of the firm's troubles. How convenient! Conceiving of themselves as patients, the EuroText leaders were quick to tell the doctors where it hurt and what to fix. In addition, they believed that no outsider or consulting team would be able to fully grasp the intricacies of their idiosyncratic organizational culture. In essence, outsiders were doomed to be outsiders. As a result, EuroText felt justified in performing its own internal investigation and expected DT&G to confirm it. In other words, the client hoped to receive rapid-fire validation of their self-diagnosis. While treading lightly during the early days of the consultation, DT&G was nevertheless initially concerned about the aggressive stance of the client.

In the client's view, its symptoms reflected a dysfunctional or toxic state of affairs that was certain to escalate. Immediately speaking, the toxicity had created an "impression management" problem. EuroText wanted DT&G to take an active role in turning around the negative press surrounding their leadership problems and provide some damage control for the eroding EuroText brand. According to the EuroText CEO, Dr. Colin Cavendish (he had earned a doctorate in business from a university in the UK), the DT&G consultants had been called in by the client "to confirm and act on the eye of the corporate storm in time to salvage what was left of leadership, personnel, and bottom lines, as well as implement a constructive impression management campaign."

The headline "DT&G Consultants Contracted by EuroText to Put Out Company Fires" instantly appeared in the company newsletter, local and international news media, and across the World Wide Web. Curiously, the media strategy was planned before the contractual ink had dried between EuroText and DT&G. Clearly, EuroText initially viewed the outside consultants as expert "doctors" who were brought on board to cure what ailed the firm. And EuroText was the overbearing, dominant, and know-it-all patient. DT&G, however, was not about to be bullied by the client.

DT&G BEGINS TO MAKE ITS MARK ON EUROTEXT CULTURE

In stark contrast to the client's expectations, Elroy Davis, principal consultant of Davis, Travis & Grambling, entered EuroText as a navigator and explorer, not a doctor. Davis's favorite consulting expression was that "consultants are anthropologists . . . we must learn to live and thrive with the gorillas in the corporate and political wilds." Davis was well schooled, internationally savvy, and open-minded. He had learned in his corporate CEO and consulting career that accessing company and leadership narratives was key to getting beyond the surface presentations of clients. Davis showed great patience, superb listening skills, empathy, and emotional intelligence. Moreover, Davis had an aversion to old-school theory X consultations, and instead encouraged the client to be an active partner in the consultation. Davis took pride in stating, "I don't give corporations hypodermic needles. Client companies have to participate in their own decisions on medications. I prescribe leadership pills and interventions, but I don't pierce the corporate skin or use the jaws of life when a CEO's in a wreck."

EuroText assuredly presented its maladies to Dr. Davis. The human resources director, Andrea Kline, stated that the problems were "centered in plunging performance, eroding quality, and a host of measurables falling into the deficit column." Closer examination of productivity levels over the previous four years revealed a pattern of negative output. There was a growing incidence of absenteeism among line workers, with scattered reports of conflict-ridden work teams, faltering morale, and the sabotaging of "bread and butter" components during the assembly process. In addition, HR reported a troubling pattern of "accelerating resistance and retaliation triggered by the strategic undermining of three beloved production managers and two supervisors, resulting in grievances, transfers, and reassignments. Consummate professionals at our Brussels plant cannot accept that esteemed colleagues were abruptly transferred to the Denver, Colorado, and Oakland, California, plants across the Atlantic—without due process or notice to their loyal work teams!"

In response, stakeholders pressed to tighten the corporate belt, reduce their losses, and control the rampant rumors circulating in Brussels. The EuroText CEO scoffed at disturbing talk that "Gravestone was growing wildly narcissistic and was a 'Queen Bee' intent on eliminating the brightest among his colleagues and competitors." The president joined the CEO in nixing this possibility while the executive board vacillated. Was a toxic senior manager at the nexus of this storm?

THE CONSULTANTS' ASSESSMENT

At the outset, EuroText expressed a desire for quick diagnosis and treatment. Not intimidated by their headstrong client, Elroy Davis and the DT&G group approached their consultations and coaching with the mindset that a differential diagnosis (see glossary) was needed. In order to conduct their discovery and data collection the consultants required a close give-and-take with the clients rather than a dictatorial briefing by the patient (see Miller 1981). Instead of producing a diagnosis that matched EuroText's, Davis arranged with the corporate client to conduct a series of comprehensive assessment interviews.

Through these interviews and field observations, Davis and his associates discovered that the drastic dip in production, rising absenteeism, sabotage, interpersonal conflict, and overall destructive behavior closely coincided with what management theorists and consultants call "toxic leadership" (see Goldman 2006a, 2006b; Kets de Vries 2006; Van Fleet and Griffin 2006). EuroText's longstanding and admired senior manager, David Gravestone, was mired in a messy public divorce and child custody case. The usually steadfast and grounded manager appeared to have lost his firm grip on EuroText's daily operations as the custody battle raged on and made headlines in Brussels, London, and other European cities. Normally a consummate professional, Gravestone was clearly not himself. He had become dismissive of his colleagues, moody, evasive, intermittently argumentative, and inclined to engage in bullying behavior with subordinates. In addition, since beginning the litigation phase of his prime-time divorce, Gravestone had spent less time as a face-to-face manager. The majority of his division expressed resentment over the behavior of their missing-in-action supervisor.

Gravestone further bewildered his colleagues by drastically altering his appearance. Known as an Ivy League–type who dressed in traditional blue blazers and khaki suits with striped ties, Gravestone abruptly changed his style. One afternoon he appeared sporting longer hair dyed jet black, a goatee, and a black and silver Elvis-style jumpsuit. He made his grand entrance in the EuroText parking lot with a shiny new red Aston Martin convertible and a young and glamorous ladyfriend. Whispers of "narcissist," "playboy," and "womanizer" floated through the hallways.

The once conservative and collaborative boss had morphed into a male peacock, primping, dashing off to upscale luncheon dates, and making the scene at trendy nightclubs and cabarets. On the job, Gravestone smiled more than ever, but was also often condescending and inconsiderate. Whenever a subordinate questioned, challenged, or looked sideways, Gravestone would adopt an imperious tone. Eliot Barrish, an IT specialist, particularly objected to "public and defacing tongue lashings" and Gravestone's "haughty facial expressions."

The leader typically went after defenseless, lower-level employees who had little recourse but to gossip and plot behind his back. On several occasions Gravestone went for the bigger fish and tied into a mid-level manager. Finally, one manager, Jules Grove, responded in kind. This heckling match swiftly led

Gravestone to transfer Grove to one of the outland offices in the United States. Through all of this, Gravestone's small inner circle of loyal subordinates and followers overwhelmingly supported their boss. CEO Cavendish offered public approval of Gravestone's "strategic reassignment of a manager who best belonged in the U.S." The executive board meekly concurred.

Gravestone's "narcissistic and agitated phase" was followed by a physical retreat. The manager who had always mingled and "micromanaged by wandering around" (MBWA; see glossary) gradually phased out his physical presence and took to text messaging and e-mailing. Gravestone's new virtual leadership style identity did not work well at EuroText. He gradually lost his iron hold over managers and staff, productivity dropped, and a whole new wave of unrest rose up among employees and colleagues.

These behaviors had been escalating for approximately eight months before the consultants were brought in. The narrative of a broken chain-of-command unfolded to the DT&G consultants through a series of structured interviews with Andrea Kline and key members of EuroText's work teams. In addition, DT&G administered 360-degree feedback (see glossary) in an effort to generate information about the workplace perception of Gravestone's leadership. The questionnaires were distributed with extremely reluctant approval from upstairs. At this stage of the consultation EuroText stepped back and assumed a more reactive role to the leadership exerted by DT&G. The consultants' attempts to involve the client were repeatedly resisted, misinterpreted, and rejected by EuroText, whose leaders proclaimed, "The outside experts have been hired to be the experts. Tell your patient what to do and we will take our medicine. But remember, the patient knows better than the doctor where it hurts!"

To say that EuroText's leaders disagreed with the data and documentation gathered by DT&G would be an understatement. DT&G told EuroText that toxic leadership behavior was increasingly recognized as a nexus in dysfunctional organizations and was addressed in a growing number of management and leadership studies (Miller and Droge 1986; Miller and Toulouse 1986; Miller, Kets de Vries, and Toulouse 1982). In extensive dialogue the consultants emphasized that "trouble at the top" necessitated serious attention. The implications were clear. The toxicity did not begin and end with Gravestone. The "toxic leadership" diagnosis extended to the CEO, president, vice president, and members of the executive board.

EuroText was not pleased. This was not what they had expected to hear. In one heated exchange, the company's newly appointed vice president, Miles

Rackman, commented sarcastically, "Please don't give me that old line that the fish rots from the head down! How naïve do you think we are? I was under the impression that we hire consultants to find causality and get to the root of the problem, not to point fingers at their clients and superiors!" In response to DT&G's needs assessment and formal report addressing toxic leadership, Euro-Text stonewalled. An impasse had been reached in the consultation. It came to a head when EuroText threatened to abort the contract with DT&G. The consultants suggested that they collectively embark with their clients on a "soul-searching mission." Faced with escalating stakeholder pressure and litigation, EuroText leadership reluctantly agreed to enter into a new conversation and search for causes and solutions.

SCRIPTING: A MORE CLIENT-CENTERED COLLABORATION

Elroy Davis told a cross-functional EuroText executive team that if they were going to move forward in the consultation it would be necessary for EuroText to face its problems side-by-side with DT&G. In order to resuscitate the client-consultant relationship, they needed a far more client-centered and collaborative effort. Finally EuroText's leadership team conceded to work according to the consultants' recommendation. After all, EuroText recognized that it had initially extended carte blanche to the consultants only to reject their "toxic leadership" findings. It finally appeared reasonable to the client to become a full-fledged player and engage in a collaborative relationship. But how was this to be achieved?

Davis, Travis & Grambling offered up a little book entitled *Getting to Yes* by Fisher, Ury, and Patton, and made a twenty-minute PowerPoint presentation about the renowned Harvard Negotiation Project (see glossary) and its impact in executive quarters around the world (Fisher, Ury, and Patton 1991; Kolb and Williams 2003). Although EuroText and DT&G initially viewed the consultation process differently, each side was willing to make concessions. Following the briefing and presentation, the EuroText CEO observed that the hostile, combative, and dysfunctional environment at the company had likely carried over into the consulting relationship. DT&G agreed that this was a real possibility. Rephrasing this revelation, the consulting group posited that sometimes "the resistance from the client mirrors and parallels the deeply rooted conflict and crisis already suffered through by the company."

Agreeing to enter into a more client-centered collaboration, the consultants provided a blueprint derived from the Harvard Negotiation Project for devel-

oping two separate and distinctive "scripts." The plan was for EuroText, in a series of soul-searching team meetings, to generate a "Top 6" list of the roots and
nature of their organizational conflict and toxic leadership. The "scripting" plan
also required that the team brainstorm options and specific interventions for
moving toward positive change. Similarly, the consulting team would prepare
its own Top 6 list. The teams would work separately for a period of three days,
during which they would have access to any and all EuroText employees who
might have a bearing on the development of the team scripts. On the fourth day
they would come together, share their scripts, agree to be nonjudgmental, and
negotiate bridges between the two scripts—collaborating to produce a hybrid
script for the consultation. In other words, working separately, both client and
consultant were to articulate what was broken at EuroText and how to fix it.
Both teams enthusiastically agreed to this scripting agenda and pursued it with
vigor and conviction. The following is an abbreviated version of the two scripts
generated.

The EuroText Script

1. Plunging productivity is due to poor hires and lazy, uncommitted workers.

2. Layoffs are a natural, fitting, and sober response to production problems,
poor quality compliance, and motivational issues.

3. The software market is in flux, and as soon as EuroText establishes its
unique brand and niche the market will turn around.

4. EuroText is waiting for a major team of German investors and a Bank of
Brussels loan to come through. These resources will be used to support activities that will lead to a major turnaround.

5. EuroText sees that some of its northern European competitors are on the
edge and will soon fold their tents and concede to EuroText.

6. EuroText's new voice activation technology will blow the lid off of the
software industry, establishing new benchmarks and solidifying long-awaited
success and innovation at our company.

Interpretation of the EuroText Script. The client-driven assessment was
not especially astute, and nowhere did EuroText address the people side of the
equation. Like a patient entering psychotherapy, EuroText was in the market
for significant business improvements, but did not want to open itself up to
difficult personal changes. In EuroText's view, its crisis was driven by a temporarily inhospitable market, a longer-than-anticipated waiting game for in-

vestors, and the failures of workers to roll up their sleeves and be productive. EuroText carefully avoided addressing leadership shortcomings, the personal problems and contested divorce of senior manager Gravestone, and the overall failures in relationship management. The company team made no mention of a deeply disturbed and distracted senior manager or of the escalating companywide arguments and toxicity emanating from Gravestone, the executive board, engineers, HR, factory line workers, and staff. Instead, its list focused on external interventions and on buying time for positive shifts by investors and the software market. The EuroText executives carefully sidestepped corporate dysfunction and failing leadership.

The DT&G team composed a starkly contrasting script.

The DT&G Consulting Script

1. The company's plunging productivity is a product of: (a) inadequate training of new employees and shortcomings and deterioration of the EuroText continuous training regimen; and (b) troubled, agitated, bullying, and absentee leadership permeating down the organizational ladder.

2. Unexpected and unexplained reassignments and transfers of popular managers have compounded and fueled plunging productivity problems, communicating a generalized companywide state of fear and imminent crisis.

3. People problems are at the core of the EuroText crisis; toxic leadership begins at the senior manager level and rises from there.

4. Training and consultation to address these people problems will require self-examination, leadership reform, and a long-overdue reorganization.

5. At the level of senior manager and above, EuroText faces leadership issues. The behavior and value of the missing-in-action David Gravestone must be carefully assessed inasmuch as his profound creativity in IT engineering is invaluable to EuroText; it is recommended that senior manager Gravestone continue with his current psychotherapy regimen and in addition begin a leadership coaching relationship with a designated member of the DT&G group.

6. Despite the fact that Gravestone increasingly acknowledges his personal issues, he is at present not amenable to rapid change or a makeover because of the personal stressors confronting him. As a result, DT&G, after considering alternatives, finds that the senior manager should be accommodated. Specifically, all marketplace and innovation concerns from the client team have their best chance of being realized through a reinstatement, reintegration, and reinvention of Gravestone. In short, it is anticipated that following leadership coaching,

psychotherapy, and the strategic changes posited in item #5 of the DT&G script the EuroText senior manager should receive a vote of confidence. Once the firm has incorporated a serious set of people adjustments as recommended by the consultants, investors and leaders will once again be able to have confidence that the firm is a winner rather than a faltering IT company.

Interpretation of the DT&G Script. In contrast to the client's script, the consultants' scenario was people- and relationship-focused, pointing out that interpersonal and toxic leadership issues were at the core of the conflict. Having anticipated that the client would be more product- and marketplace-driven in its script, the consultants decided to emphasize the leaders' dysfunctional behavior in a constructive manner. Foremost in the consultants' script were their views of the allegedly toxic senior manager, Gravestone. Gravestone's rather unusual role as both a long-term top R&D engineer and senior manager, combined with his turbulent and very public divorce, provided a profile for potential professional and personal stress.

After carefully considering all the information it had gathered, the consulting team determined that the long-term R&D contributions of Gravestone to his company outweighed the deficits. Gravestone had been an exemplary innovator, and he would most likely prove pivotal in the reconstruction of EuroText's research division and overall brand. Accordingly, the consulting team decided to brainstorm with the client team about ways their top shop leader could reemerge as a groundbreaking R&D engineering innovator and also retain his leadership role. Although Gravestone was not in a position to radically alter his recent behavior, by modifying the hierarchy, the corporate goals could be served.

REINVENTING THE TOXIC MANAGER:
NEGOTIATION AND INTERVENTION

The submission and exchange of the scripts between client and consultant was followed by a second three-day incubation period. On day four the two teams met to discuss each other's scripts. The ground rules stipulated that there be no initial judgments, just a consideration of all points raised in the two scripts.

The consultants suggested that Marcus Washburn, a sober, pragmatic, and successful EuroText mid-level manager and administrator in the quality assurance program, be designated as a "right-hand man" to Gravestone. It was suggested that the strength, clarity, and administrative smarts of Washburn would complement and enhance the innovative but unpredictable and recently toxic behavior of Gravestone. The external experts convincingly illustrated the creative worth of Gravestone, as well as his role in EuroText's earlier successes.

EuroText was impressed by the insights of the consultants and pleasantly surprised by their assessments and recommended intervention. The client appreciated the humanity and insight of the DT&G consultants, which did not compromise their hopes for investors, loans, and an IT niche market. Negotiations led to Gravestone participating in a DT&G-directed program entitled "Leader Detox Training." In addition, a serious self-examination led the EuroText leadership to recognize that they had been guilty of acute avoidance of the people issues and also ineffective and negligent in their companywide response to Gravestone's difficulties. Gravestone himself was quite pleased with the outcome. Collectively, EuroText and DT&G discussed whether a permanent restructuring of the hierarchy might be in order, under the supervision of the senior management team of Gravestone and Washburn.

Through a negotiation process, a hybrid of the two scripts was achieved. It incorporated the product- and market-driven analysis of the client, as well as the emotionally intelligent insights of DT&G. Most important was the fact that, although DT&G had structured the consultation, the final results and relationships were thoroughly client-driven. DT&G had had to exert little pressure on the clients to adopt the consultants' script. Once buy-in was achieved on the scripting agenda, the ensuing wide-ranging brainstorming and negotiation process led to genuinely hybrid ideas for interventions. Of special note was the realization on the part of the EuroText team that despite the substantive differences in the two scripts, their underlying interests were quite compatible. Both client and consultants wanted to save EuroText and believed that Gravestone's innovations held the key despite his recent digressions.

Central to the negotiation process was the enthusiastic reception and acceptance of the restructuring by both David Gravestone and Marcus Washburn. In a candid moment with a DT&G leadership coach, Gravestone confided, "I would welcome a period of at least twelve to eighteen months to get the divorce settled and get my head back together. I also need at least a year or so to continue with therapy and meds. . . . I have been frazzled to say the least, and I am privately embarrassed by my behavior at EuroText. A chilling-out period would be sweet." The final composite document following a series of rewrites and drafts was unanimously adopted by the EuroText team in approximately

fifteen minutes following a public reading at the negotiating table. In the esti-
mation of the EuroText team this document was 75 percent client-driven; the
earlier dissonance and conflict with DT&G had led to a genuine soul-searching
and a 360-degree comprehension of their crisis.

CONSULTATION RESULTS

The culmination of the restructuring of the EuroText R&D division was
a "smooth interim period," with Washburn assuming the bulk of the senior
manager duties and Gravestone serving in an advisory capacity as a "shadow
manager."

During the interim period the chronic absentee rate dropped from a high
of 19 percent to a reasonable 2 percent; three of the previously transferred managers were brought back to the Brussels office, a move that dramatically raised
trust in the division and improved its collaborative teamwork; 87 percent of the
grievances against Gravestone were settled by the EuroText HR director and
ombudsperson; and the new leadership partnership between Gravestone and
Washburn was rated extremely highly in 360-degree feedback during month
thirteen of the transition.

Also during the interim period the company launched four major innovations, three of which Gravestone was instrumental in developing and op-
erationalizing, including the long-anticipated voice activation system. Productivity went up dramatically, as did motivation. At the close of the designated
eighteen-month period, Gravestone concluded therapy with his psychologist
and continued on with leadership coaching with DT&G. Also at the eighteen-
month milestone, Gravestone's divorce was finalized and he received joint custody of his two children, ages twelve and fifteen. At the twenty-two-month mark
Gravestone was appointed vice president of a new Special Projects division. A
new and relaxed Gravestone returned to his traditional conservative dress and
traded in his Aston Martin convertible for a Nissan Maxima hardtop.

COMMENTARY

EuroText, a firm with a complex organizational system, entered into a customized and evolving consulting relationship with the DT&G group. Overcoming client resistance and an overly protective and defensive stance toward their
senior manager, the consultants proceeded with a thoroughly differential diagnosis and a multi-dimensional consultation. Faced with a highly toxic senior
manager receiving psychological care and going through a difficult divorce, the

consultants weighed the wisdom of "removing the rotten apple from the barrel." Extensive companywide assessment led to the conclusion that EuroText had too much to lose by dismissing Gravestone.

Rather than accepting the onslaught of grievances levied by employees against the senior manager and dismissing him, DT&G chose to treat Gravestone as an innovative and valuable asset to EuroText who was going through a traumatic personal time. Rather than dwelling on "deficit gaps" in the senior manager's behavior and in the plight of EuroText, the consultants reconceptualized the toxicity as an "abundance gap." In working toward a positive transformation of the senior manager and his company, they collaborated with the client to develop an interim restructuring experiment that provided Gravestone with a formal vote of confidence at a time when he was suffering from low self-efficacy.

The trust, empathy, and compassion afforded Gravestone via the consultation and intervention were instrumental in his eventual positive transformation from a dysfunctional to a functional leader, and eventually into a highly effective and respected leader of the new Special Projects division.

Central to the transformation of both leader and organization was the ability of DT&G to bring a consulting stalemate into a Harvard Negotiation Project–inspired negotiation. In the process the defensiveness and resistance of the client's top leaders and their initial desire for a hierarchical relationship was transformed into an empowered and horizontal partnership with the DT&G consultants.

A HEALTHY CLIENT-CONSULTANT RELATIONSHIP

Even successful assessments and interventions are laced with significant problems, challenges, and conflicts. The exemplary consultation prioritizes relationship and interpersonal processes and recognizes that customized and innovative interventions are highly contingent upon client involvement. The development and nurturing of active collaboration and engagement of the client is a nexus in high-impact consultations. What emerges is a positioning of the client as a central agent in consultations; it is a complex composite of "the client" quite separate and apart from typical images of client naiveté (see Gallesich 1982; Sturdy 1997).

In this consultation, EuroText initially approached DT&G with some preformed ideas about the relationship between client and consultant. The firm's leaders saw the consultants as doctors who would confirm the organization's own diagnosis of its illness and provide behavioral interventions to heal the pain. The consultants figuratively rolled their eyes and politely dismissed the client's expectations. But as often happens, once the external expert diagnoses the real cause of the illness and prescribes a treatment, the client resists. In response to DT&G's initial assessment of the client's illness, EuroText became defensive, attempting to insulate and protect leadership. Through an extensive dialogue and negotiating process, the consultation was rescued, and together the client and consultants were able to work toward their common goal, with the clients as active participants.

6 Leader Detoxification: Strategies for Transforming Toxic Leaders and Organizations

It is true that good leadership by its very nature engenders pain. It pushes people out of their comfort zones—which is necessary to get things done in a world of competition and change. Even so, some managers are malicious or lack good decision-making or people-managing skills, and therefore unduly contribute to the frustration, anger and low morale of their employees. . . . Not just managers but organizations themselves create conditions for toxicity through policies and practices that fail to include the human factor in their execution.

—P. Frost, *Toxic Emotions in the Workplace*

As a leadership coach and management consultant I naturally expect to learn life lessons from every client. Here I take stock and catalogue what can be gleaned from the trials and tribulations of the toxic leaders and organizations whose stories are told in the preceding chapters. The unifying theme is, of course, transforming toxic leaders through *detoxification*. Detoxification is the umbrella term for directly addressing dysfunctional decisions, policies, oversights, miscalculations, avoidance behavior, and leadership and follower behaviors that contaminate employees and operations. Business-as-usual cannot respond to toxicity; it requires a resourceful and carefully constructed systemic plan. Detoxification is an ongoing process. The strategies presented here offer benchmarks and prototypes for leaders and organizations everywhere in dealing with toxic environments caused by demagogic leadership, downsizing, feuding between employees, post-traumatic stress and burnout, and emotional trauma.

In this chapter I go beyond information, theory, and assessment. It is my intention to not only open the doors to the underlying causes and roots of destructive leaders and policies, but also to provide a blueprint for empowering companies to take action through detoxification strategies.

DETOXIFICATION STRATEGIES

Toxic leaders and policies are the opposite of positive organizational behavior. They invite diagnosis and intervention. Faced with organizational conflict, decline in financial and psychological capital, and an inability to assess or intervene in a timely way, the leaders of Bentley Pacific, North Country Solutions, SkyWaves Aerospace, Eisenhower Heart Institute, Jarling-Weber, and EuroText turned to external management consultants and leadership coaches. My examination of these consultations has produced 125 strategies and interventions for assessing, controlling, and transforming toxicity into more operational and positive behaviors.

What follows is a chapter-by-chapter discussion of the principles of detoxification. A short recapitulation of the "toxic essence" of each consultation is followed by a point-by-point list of detoxification strategies. Leaders and organizations can use these strategies to intervene in toxic circumstances contingent upon the conditions and variables described. The detoxification interventions presented are representative of the toxicities experienced in a myriad of organizations. Immediately following the detoxification strategies I provide a synthesis and blueprint for action.

DETOX ONE: DEMAGOGUE TO DIALOGUE

The demagogic, leader-by-edict approach of Bentley CEO Cal Burton described in Chapter 1 is classic behavior in the prototypical hierarchical or vertical organizational culture. Caught in the midst of an abrupt and radical downsizing, Bentley Pacific employees responded to their demagogic leader with an arsenal of retaliatory measures. The toxic environment was compounded by hostility and incivility from the CEO, symptomatic of a DSM IV-TR disorder, intermittent explosive disorder, a not unusual affliction among Fortune 500 corporate leaders.

In contrast, Lane Blake, CEO of North Country Solutions, took a prototypically dialogue- and relationship-rich approach to a downsizing. The highly successful Blake saw lower levels of dysfunction and toxicity in her firm and engaged a developmental leadership coach. They addressed these low levels of negative organizational behavior because Blake hoped to secure downside protection and ward off more serious levels of toxicity.

Toxin 1.1   Abrupt dismissals, hires, and other changes in senior leadership. **Detox 1.1** requires companywide communication and preparation for strategic changes in leadership.

Toxin 1.2   Dramatic differences in personality and leadership style between an outgoing and an incoming leader. **Detox 1.2** requires less rather than more disparity between an outgoing leader and the new one.

Toxin 1.3   When interviewing a candidate for a leadership appointment, a firm's failure to thoroughly screen the candidate, within the limits of the law, for preexisting emotional or psychological issues and disorders. **Detox 1.3** requires developing a 360-degree companywide commitment to uncovering any preexisting psychological conditions in a potential leadership hire.

Toxin 1.4   Failure to achieve high-order collaboration and communication among all of the entities concerned with the hiring and selection of an incoming leader. **Detox 1.4.** In the hiring process, avoid letting anyone make a hiring decision unilaterally; work toward high-level communication and coordination among all of the players involved in the interviewing and selection process.

Toxin 1.5   Attempts by people without specialized training to diagnose mental or emotional disturbances. **Detox 1.5.** Leaders acting as coaches and counselors are best equipped to determine "normal" toxic levels of everyday conflict in the workplace. It is recommended that organizations designate a qualified internal professional or support person to determine the severity of conflicts in the workplace and suggest appropriate treatment avenues (requires DSM knowledge and a master's degree in social work or psychology, or counseling and clinical psychology training).

Toxin 1.6   Failure to respond in a timely manner to conflict-ridden and emotionally painful leadership. **Detox 1.6.** Confidential, open-door, and user-friendly policies and procedures for addressing conflict, fears, perceived threats, and emotionally painful experiences with leadership should be provided by superiors, managers, HR, and the EAP.

Toxin 1.7   Management's failure to anticipate the organizational challenges they will face in response to psychological disturbances in the workplace. **Detox 1.7.** Anticipate privileged communication and the inability to access information about leaders who might receive DSM diagnoses (see American Psychiatric Association 2000). Have company attorneys review the range of responses permitted within the limits of the law to leaders who exercise confidentiality following diagnoses of psychological disorders.

Toxin 1.8   Downsizings that focus primarily on cost-cutting measures and are unaccompanied by emotionally competent communication with both employees being fired and those being retained. **Detox 1.8.** Ongoing development, refinement, and prioritizing of people skills, emotional intelligence, and right-brain communication in synch with cost-containment measures will significantly deescalate toxicity in a downsizing.

Toxin 1.9   Demagoguery by any name. **Detox 1.9.** Toxicity can be reduced through dialogue and collaboration, which flatten steep, top-down decision-making.

Toxin 1.10   Leaders who go it alone in responding to employee conflicts, fears, and high levels of stress. **Detox 1.10.** The leader who wants to play the role of toxin detector and healer will do best to collaborate with HR, employee assistant program counselors, and psychotherapists when interacting with employees in a highly troubled workplace.

DETOX TWO: EMOTIONAL DEPOSITS AND WITHDRAWALS

As described in Chapter 2, the "leave your emotions at the door" culture of SkyWaves Aerospace fueled a conflict between two engineers in the R&D division. Extreme avoidance behavior on the part of the HR director and the R&D division head allowed a once manageable dispute to smolder and grow toxic over a six-year period, negatively affecting productivity, morale, teamwork, innovation, and relationships in the workplace. An alarming number of requests by engineers to relocate within the SkyWaves system left the R&D division in a seriously diminished and compromised state. After the new HR director's efforts fell short, an external consultant was brought in well into the "ninth inning" of the toxicity.

Toxin 2.1   Lack of leadership responsiveness to and/or avoidance of workplace conflicts. **Detox 2.1.** Leaders who function in the internal coach, consultant, and counselor capacities enhance the prospect for detecting and deflating conflict before it escalates and turns toxic.

Toxin 2.2   An unwritten "no emotions allowed" policy in the workplace. **Detox 2.2.** An atmosphere that encourages emotional expression can diminish interpersonal, relational, and superior-subordinate toxicity in the workplace.

Toxin 2.3   Escalating numbers of employee requests to transfer to other locations within the organization may result in a "human turnstile." **Detox 2.3.** Leadership should investigate possible objective and emotional triggers of transfer requests, prioritizing how people and relationship issues may have contributed to job dissatisfaction, loss of hope, and pessimism. The opening of dialogue to unravel the underlying problems and causes will support organizational detoxification.

Toxin 2.4   Annual performance appraisals that emphasize tasks, objective criteria, and measurables without recognizing relationship and emotional competency. **Detox 2.4.** Quarterly (or preferably monthly) performance management interviews that focus on relationship and emotional competency minimize or reduce interpersonal toxicity.

Toxin 2.5   Leaders who ignore employees' (and their own) emotional side—dreams, fears, aspirations, and visions. **Detox 2.5.** A leader who acknowledges the right-brain, emotional side of operating in the workplace can help to prevent organizational toxicity.

Toxin 2.6   Neglecting to respond to an ordinary altercation between two employees. **Detox 2.6.** Leaders who respond to everyday workplace conflicts in a timely and emotionally competent way facilitate conflict resolution.

Toxin 2.7   Leaders who focus, consciously or unconsciously, intentionally or unintentionally, on left-brain (logical, scientific, measurable, task-oriented) behavior. **Detox 2.7.** Development of right-brain (intuitive, emotional, poetic, innovative) leadership behavior may be a source of organizational detoxification.

Toxin 2.8   Leaders who believe that emotions are unpredictable, messy, and base-level expressions of a less educated and more primitive mammal. **Detox 2.8.** The belief that emotional intelligence and emotional competency are at the nexus of strong leadership and motivated employees can be a source of organizational detoxification.

Toxin 2.9   Leaders who say, "Don't go soft on me and expose my managers to this mushy people stuff." **Detox 2.9.** Leaders with emotional intelligence make possible what Whetten and Cameron (2007) call "emotional deposits" into the accounts of colleagues, a source of organizational detoxification.

Toxin 2.10   Leaders who ignore toxic emotions until they are unavoidable and undeniable. **Detox 2.10.** Acknowledging that negative emotions have infiltrated and poisoned the workplace is an essential step toward organizational detoxification.

Toxin 2.11   A narrow emphasis on dissecting and emulating successful leadership and positive organizational behavior accompanied by an avoidance of destructive and toxic dimensions of management. **Detox 2.11.** Ample and timely addressing of toxic leadership and policies requires a more balanced view of the workplace and a readiness to assess, troubleshoot, and intervene in the face of seemingly destructive behavior.

Toxin 2.12   A ninth-inning response to employee conflict. **Detox 2.12.** Timely, responsive monitoring of workplace conflicts is preventive and consistent with organizational detoxification.

Toxin 2.13   Rude and volatile workplace interactions. **Detox 2.13.** Leadership should provide supportive communication and timely ongoing troubleshooting on-the-floor to defuse hostile interactions.

Toxin 2.14   Plunging productivity and profits in one division. **Detox 2.14.** Monitoring, support, dialogue, and timely responses to dips in productivity align leadership with organizational detoxification.

Toxin 2.15   The failure of an outgoing HR director to brief an incoming HR director on existing conflict and dysfunctional behavior. **Detox 2.15.** Clear and focused policy addressing the necessity of communicating any conflict or dysfunctional behavior during a transfer of power is central to organizational detoxification.

Toxin 2.16   Unacceptable conflict, backbiting behavior, and a culture of intolerance. **Detox 2.16.** The prepared toxin detector and handler provides counseling for conflict, intolerance, and negative behavior.

Toxin 2.17   The leader who doesn't buy into "the whole people conflict psychological thing" and focuses on task, productivity, and profits. **Detox 2.17.** The well-balanced leader attempts to pay attention to people conflicts as a way to motivate employees, boost morale, and foster stability in the workplace.

Toxin 2.18 A misunderstanding or conflict between two employees that escalates and spreads. **Detox 2.18.** The leader who addresses conflicts as they arise and attempts to negotiate workable resolutions is engaged in organizational detoxification.

Toxin 2.19 Leaders who ignore unresolved employee conflicts characterized by public humiliation and loss of face in the workplace. **Detox 2.19.** Leaders should enforce policies that prohibit ad hominem attacks on coworkers and provide internal mediation, coaching, and counseling for conflict resolution.

Toxin 2.20 A lack of respect from colleagues and/or superiors that undermines employees' confidence, individual identity, and self-efficacy. **Detox 2.20.** An organizational culture that fosters respect between leadership and colleagues and that values the individual fosters positive organizational sentiments and behaviors (hope, optimism, self-efficacy, and resilience).

Toxin 2.21 Psychological diagnoses of individuals in the workplace by those who are unqualified to provide them. **Detox 2.21.** Internal company trainers or external consultants can educate leadership and employees about some of the differences between ordinary conflicts and emotional disturbances and more pathological behavior typically diagnosed by clinical professionals according to the DSM IV-TR (*Diagnostic and Statistical Manual of the American Psychiatric Association*). Employees must refrain from publicly voicing flippant and uninformed psychological diagnoses of colleagues, and clinical assessments should be left to qualified professionals. The education of leaders and employees in this arena is vital in organizational detoxification.

Toxin 2.22 Colleagues who are unable to engage in constructive dialogue over conflicts. **Detox 2.22.** Leadership trained in conflict resolution, mediation, emotional intelligence, and relationship management can open lines of communication between warring parties.

Toxin 2.23 A formal or informal policy that does not acknowledge and value the emotional intelligence dimensions of behavior. **Detox 2.23.** An ongoing and respectful dialogue about the place of emotional expression (positive and negative) in the workplace is a source of organizational detoxification.

Toxin 2.24   The strategic use of the EAP (employee assistance program) as the "local dumping ground" for negative human capital issues. **Detox 2.24.** Leaders should be alert to developing relationship issues in their departments. Healthy leadership provides supportive communication and feedback to employees locally on an as-needed basis, before referring them to the EAP.

Toxin 2.25   Public disclosure of an employee's psychological disorder in violation of the Americans with Disabilities Act (ADA) as it pertains to protected and privileged communication. **Detox 2.25.** Unless otherwise indicated via a clinician's directions, full confidentiality and privileged communication status must be maintained when employees receive a diagnosis of a psychological disorder. Leaders should promote discretion and respect in the workplace and provide private venues for communication of sensitive issues.

Toxin 2.26   Leaders who react to dysfunctional behavior rather than anticipating it. **Detox 2.26.** Organizations should develop a blueprint for handling potential dysfunctional behavior in the workplace.

DETOX THREE: LIFE-AND-DEATH LEADERSHIP

In Chapter 3, I described a brilliant and world-renowned heart surgeon specializing in mitral valve repair whose actions were the subject of controversy, hostility, and altercations throughout the cardiology division of the Eisenhower Heart Institute. Faced with potentially damaging and abusive behavior at the surgical table, the threat of life-and-death mistakes during open-heart surgery, and fear of malpractice and litigation, upper echelon leadership contracted with a management consultant and leadership coach. Although all fingers initially pointed to Dr. Ivan Lorimer as the single cause of the toxicity, the consultant uncovered multiple causes throughout the system. Two of the more pressing precipitators of the toxicity were a poorly conceived and executed corporate restructuring and inadequate, delayed, and inappropriate responses to the disputes surrounding the surgeon at the operating table.

Toxin 3.1   Abrupt, overnight, and complete-overhaul-approach to organizational restructurings. **Detox 3.1.** A restructuring that takes a gradual and incremental approach is less toxic than radical organizational change and will find more willing and flexible supporters.

Toxin 3.2   Restructurings that do not closely match the organizational and professional culture. **Detox 3.2.** When restructurings are carefully considered for organizational and cultural "fit" the risk of toxicity is greatly reduced.

Toxin 3.3   External trainers and/or consultants who, because they are not sufficiently integrated into an organization's professional culture, are perceived to be naive or hostile. **Detox 3.3.** External agents/consultants/coaches should be carefully introduced and integrated into the organizational and professional culture.

Toxin 3.4   Relationship and emotional intelligence failures in organizational restructurings. **Detox 3.4.** The integration of collaborative communication, relationship building, and emotional competency in organizational restructurings minimizes the potential for toxicity.

Toxin 3.5   A theory X (demagogic, top-down) approach to organizational restructuring. **Detox 3.5.** A collaborative, bottom-up approach to organizational restructuring that prioritizes relationship building and maximizes dialogue diminishes the likelihood of toxicity.

Toxin 3.6   An "I-It" (Buber 1965, 1970) approach to restructuring, whereby leadership treats employees as inanimate objects or widgets. **Detox 3.6.** An "I-Thou" (Buber 1970) approach to restructuring, whereby leadership maximizes employee feedback and places the highest value and priority on their personal and professional viewpoints, maximizes ownership and buy-in during restructurings.

Toxin 3.7   Outside consultants who don't distinguish between "task" and "relationship" goals during a restructuring. **Detox 3.7.** Direct and clear valuing of process and relationship goals during a restructuring reduces the incidence of workplace toxicity.

Toxin 3.8   A hit-and-run approach by external consultants whereby reports and training are considered "deliverables" and not integrated into daily operations. **Detox 3.8.** Removal of implementation gaps and a hands-on integration of new skills into daily operations limits resistance to change and renews organizational health.

Toxin 3.9   Publicly communicated leadership resistance to organizational change introduced by external consultants. **Detox 3.9.** Consultants should conduct timely dialogue with a disgruntled leader who expresses overt opposition and resistance to restructuring.

Toxin 3.10   A one-size-fits-all approach to organizational restructuring and empowerment. **Detox 3.10.** The culture of a cardiology division in a hospital is radically different from the culture of an automobile plant. A restructuring should reflect the professional culture of the organization.

Toxin 3.11   Professional/surgical table conflicts that are not immediately acknowledged and dealt with. **Detox 3.11.** Timely, comprehensive responses to and dialogue surrounding professional conflict lower toxicity and are a source of detoxification.

Toxin 3.12   Failure to respond in a timely manner to professional grievances. **Detox 3.12.** A thoroughly responsive and timely 360-degree dialogue over professional grievances lowers toxicity levels and provides impetus for detoxification.

Toxin 3.13   Failure of leadership to generate "buy-in" from professionals and employees before hiring external trainers for purposes of a restructuring. **Detox 3.13.** The use of a collaborative theory Y approach rather than a demagogic theory X approach to hiring external consultants detoxifies the process.

Toxin 3.14   Allowing a leader to publicly lose face at a meeting of professionals, colleagues, and employees. **Detox 3.14.** Policies that explicitly prohibit public humiliation of colleagues provide protection against base-level negative emotional contagion. Leaders who are present should immediately terminate personal attacks when they occur.

Toxin 3.15   Belatedly expressing support for a valued leader who has been publicly humiliated. **Detox 3.15.** Leadership must arrest dysfunctional and toxic behavior ASAP, before it does irreparable damage to workplace relationships.

DETOX FOUR: POST-TRAUMATIC LEADERSHIP

Following an abrupt, abusive, and hostile downsizing announced via e-mail, senior operations manager Max Lunger was designated by Jarling-Weber to "whip the remaining employees into shape as they grow into time-and-a-half, 150 percent work schedules" (see Chapter 4). Traumatized by a massive firing and the accompanying manhandling of remaining professionals, the post-downsizing turnover rate of approximately 38 percent sent signals to the top leadership that the company was becoming toxic. The red flag was raised after Jarling-Weber's employee assistance program diagnosed several employees with post-traumatic stress disorder. The leaders were furious with the EAP for its "idiotic assessments of do-nothing employees." Turning to the Goldstone Consulting Group, together the top leaders exhorted the external experts "stop the bleeding as soon as is humanly possible and light a fire under the lazy behinds of our programmers and all of the rest of them." Most of all, they demanded that Goldstone "invalidate, humiliate, and exorcise the abominable, slandering work of their EAP counselors."

Toxin 4.1	Lack of preparedness for traumatic events ranging from burnout, downsizings, abrupt restructurings, and hostile takeovers to abusive behavior and workplace violence. **Detox 4.1.** Preparation for trauma softens the blow of toxicity and serves as a means of organizational detoxification.
Toxin 4.2	The deceit of an external consultant by an organization or its leadership. **Detox 4.2.** Appropriate disclosure and full honesty between the client and the consultant or coach facilitates cooperation and reduces the likelihood of toxicity in the relationship.
Toxin 4.3	A firm's inability and/or failure to address the emotional, psychological, and personal dimensions of a downsizing. **Detox 4.3.** A firm that prepares its employees for release through career counseling and developmental and/or clinical coaching decreases the incidence of trauma and minimizes organizational detoxification.
Toxin 4.4	An authoritarian leadership style after a mass downsizing. **Detox 4.4.** A dialogic, relationship-building approach to leading employees retained after a mass downsizing lowers the fear level and facilitates organizational detoxification.

Toxin 4.5 Putting tasks, productivity, and profits ahead of emotional intelligence during and after a downsizing. **Detox 4.5.** Leaders should give emotional intelligence and emotional competency the highest priority during and after a downsizing.

Toxin 4.6 Leaders who are inaccessible to traumatized employees. **Detox 4.6.** Management must open its doors to and communicate with employees after a downsizing.

Toxin 4.7 Grievances and lawsuits that result from a leadership failure to engage in supportive communication and feedback during a time of crisis. **Detox 4.7.** Timely, responsive feedback to employees' complaints lessens the incidence of grievances and negative feedback.

Toxin 4.8 A coercive, intimidating approach to requiring employee overtime. **Detox 4.8.** The leader who communicates emotional competency in explaining the need for overtime makes use of lateral input from employees, enhances the credibility of leadership, lowers the prospect of burnout, and raises the probability of successful organizational detoxification after a downsizing.

Toxin 4.9 Emotional incompetence among leaders, demonstrated by premature referrals by HR, supervisors, or management to an employee assistance program for counseling or clinical coaching. **Detox 4.9.** Supervisors, managers, and HR officials must be prepared to provide coaching and counseling to employees during times of stress.

Toxin 4.10 Leaders who focus exclusively on workplace strategy and tasks and leave HR, EAP, and external contractors to deal with their employees' emotional and psychological needs. **Detox 4.10.** A firm that incorporates "toxin detectors" and "toxin healers" among its managerial ranks provides powerful signals that it supports its employees' emotional health.

Toxin 4.11 A firm that places complete faith in the "EAP option" for exhausted or burned out employees. **Detox 4.11.** Options other than the EAP should be considered when employees complain and express discontent with existing services. Dialogue coaching and clinical counseling are sources of organizational detoxification.

Toxin 4.12 A growing number of MIA (missing-in-action) employees in the workplace. **Detox 4.12.** Loss of morale, commitment, enthusiasm, and long-term patterns of tardiness and absenteeism must be addressed in a timely and emotionally competent fashion by superiors, HR, and leadership as part of a fact-finding mission and as part of the healing process.

Toxin 4.13   Turnover in work teams immediately following an abrupt downsizing. **Detox 4.13.** Astute leadership recognizes that team and job assignments are in a state of flux following a downsizing and that employees may find it difficult to sustain their commitment to work groups. Dialogue and a timely addressing of work-team conflicts is a step toward organizational detoxification.

Toxin 4.14   Leaders who avoid or do not respond to employees who have been traumatized by workplace events. **Detox 4.14.** Timely superior-subordinate dialogue about traumatic and emotionally difficult workplace events, along with appropriate referral to internal or external experts, can deescalate organizational toxicity.

Toxin 4.15   Companywide efforts to suppress talk about the root causes of a radical downsizing and restructuring. **Detox 4.15.** Open discussion, dialogue, and discovery addressing root causes of a downsizing empower employees during times of extreme stress and provide a source of organizational detoxification.

Toxin 4.16   Holding up workaholic overtimers as high achievers. **Detox 4.16.** Not all employees are in a position to take on additional work, either psychologically or in their personal circumstances. Leadership's acknowledgment of stress, failing health, and relationship problems associated with burnout is central to opening a dialogue.

Toxin 4.17   Employees with a strong self-preservation instinct who are driven to work extremely long hours. **Detox 4.17.** In a culture of fear following a downsizing, leadership may want to direct high-productivity and overtime objectives more toward teams than individuals.

Toxin 4.18   Leaders who distrust their EAP and reject its diagnoses of employees' psychological problems. **Detox 4.18.** Constructive dialogue among management, leadership, HR, and the EAP raises the level of trust and the potential for collaboration.

Toxin 4.19   Management's hiring of an external consulting/coaching expert to counter "the poisonous effect of EAP sabotage" and "faulty diagnoses." **Detox 4.19.** The hiring of an external consulting/coaching expert to conduct a needs assessment and discover the real sources of toxicity and dysfunction between departments is a step in the direction of organizational detoxification.

Toxin 4.20 Leadership's proclamation that "burnout" is a meaningless and politically correct term to describe employees who are unmotivated, weak, and looking for excuses. **Detox 4.20.** Leadership's ability to deal with the threat, realization or reality of burnout in an emotionally intelligent ongoing dialogue is a step toward organizational detoxification.

Toxin 4.21 A senior manager's refusal to assume any personal or organizational responsibility for employee burnout and low morale. **Detox 4.21.** Senior managers should publicly acknowledge that personal issues such as employee burnout are a fact of the workplace and address them in a timely, constructive, and professional manner.

Toxin 4.22 Organizational dysfunction caused by burnout. **Detox 4.22.** Leadership must actively address the correlation between burnout and organizational dysfunction.

Toxin 4.23 Trying to turbocharge productivity by dangling cash benefits and carrots in the faces of employees and simultaneously mocking and demeaning those who don't go for the bait. **Detox 4.23.** An optimistic and confidence-building approach to company rejuvenation and entertaining new overtime options promotes organizational detoxification.

Toxin 4.24 Productivity that is achieved through coercion and leads to employee burnout. **Detox 4.24.** After a downsizing, a longer-range and empowerment approach to renewal is preferable to the imposition of leadership-by-fear-and-edict.

Toxin 4.25 A client who tells the consultant that a needs assessment is not necessary because its employees are lazy and need to be micromanaged. **Detox 4.25.** Allowing the consultant to conduct a needs assessment is a first step toward organizational detoxification.

Toxin 4.26 A client that contracts with a consultant in order to validate its own dysfunctional behavior and decisions. **Detox 4.26.** The consultant should refuse to accept unethical and dysfunctional conditions at the onset of a consultation.

Toxin 4.27   A long-term pattern of top-down control characterized by distrust of outsiders, hidden motives and agendas, and distortions of reality. **Detox 4.27.** Leadership must be ready to accept a diagnosis and agree to interventions recommended by the consultant.

Toxin 4.28   A consultant's failure to address individual leadership issues. **Detox 4.28.** External experts should consider whether executive or leadership assistance would be beneficial to a client. Such assistance could be in the form of developmental coaching (to strengthen leadership capacity) or clinical coaching (to provide psychological support).

DETOX FIVE: REINVENTING THE TOXIC LEADER

As described in Chapter 5, a brilliant and longstanding senior manager for EuroText, David Gravestone, went through what employees termed a "toxic metamorphosis." The once highly personable leader with boundless energy became an absentee leader. He rarely appeared at the office. When he did, his behavior was increasingly inappropriate and erratic. It was public knowledge that Gravestone was undergoing a contested divorce and child custody battle. Over a period of just a few months Gravestone radically altered his physical appearance, bought a red sports car, and began squiring "inappropriately dressed" lady friends.

Rather than acknowledge and work with Gravestone's increasingly toxic behavior, the president and executive board blamed mounting workplace problems on employees and attempted to utilize the DT&G consultants to validate their unfounded perceptions. But when the consultants saw things differently, a conflict ensued. Using techniques and strategies developed by the Harvard Negotiation Project, and attempting to reframe the many talents of Gravestone, the consultants proposed a restructuring whereby Gravestone would be able to survive his personal storms. A new leadership partnership elevated a respected company executive and allowed Gravestone to eventually flourish again.

Toxin 5.1   Personnel and people problems that cannot be adequately addressed, managed, or resolved internally. **Detox 5.1.** Contracting with an external management consultant and leadership coach for assistance in dealing with conflict symbolically sends a message of concern and commitment to detoxification.

Toxin 5.2   Leaders who view the external consultant and leadership coach as a "hired hand." **Detox 5.2.** Leaders should be encouraged to view the consultant/coach as an expert who will collaborate with the committed client to troubleshoot, diagnose, and intervene for positive change.

Toxin 5.3   The top-down, demagogic approach of blaming team conflict and personnel problems primarily on employees. **Detox 5.3.** A companywide assessment involving dialogue and collaboration can have a detoxifying effect.

Toxin 5.4   A leadership that views itself as immune to and separate from workplace conflict when employees' perceptions are otherwise. **Detox 5.4.** Open dialogue should explore the roots of conflict, absenteeism, bullying, and faltering productivity and profits.

Toxin 5.5   A client's passive expectation that the external consultant or leadership coach will diagnose and treat the problems without input from the organization. **Detox 5.5.** The detoxification process can only get under way when the organization and consultants/coaches form a partnership.

Toxin 5.6   Treating consultations between external coaches and corporate clients as "privileged communication" reserved for executives and leadership only. **Detox 5.6.** Appropriate levels of dialogue, disclosure, and transparency surrounding executive and leadership experiences with external experts may serve to detoxify the client-consultant relationship in the eyes of an organization's workforce.

Toxin 5.7   Waiting until organizational bleeding (via transfers, grievances, and litigation) reaches a crisis level before calling in an external consultant. **Detox 5.7.** Leaders should consider contracting with an external consultant or coach during the early stages of workplace conflict.

Toxin 5.8   A leader whose repeated absences are unexplained. **Detox 5.8.** A leader who is candid and transparent about the reasons for his absenteeism or other unexpected behavior will minimize toxicity.

Toxin 5.9   Use of consultants to turn around a negative corporate image without addressing related behavioral issues. **Detox 5.9.** Clients and consultants should collaborate to identify and remedy all the sources of a company's negative image.

Toxin 5.10   Failure of the external consultant or coach to conduct a needs assessment before proceeding with an intervention. A client should not conduct its own needs assessment and present it to the consultant. (Gallesich 1982) **Detox 5.10.** Consultant and client must collaborate during a "discovery period" and the joint pursuit of a diagnosis.

Toxin 5.11   Leadership's failure to explain dismissals of well-liked and respected employees. **Detox 5.11.** Open dialogue and a flattened, more horizontal approach to dismissals characterized by appropriate levels of input from various levels within the organization and/or transparency to people at all levels serves organizational detoxification.

Toxin 5.12   Consultant or coaching interventions that are undertaken rapidly, without comprehensive diagnostic interviews and a needs assessment. **Detox 5.12.** Although there is a school of thought that advocates rapid implementation of consultants' recommendations, organizational detoxification is best served by attempting to situate incremental consults within the context of a broader systems or differential diagnosis.

Toxin 5.13   Attempts to avoid, overlook, or separate a leader's personal traumas from leadership in the workplace. **Detox 5.13.** The proactive detection and acknowledgment of leaders' personal difficulties is mandatory; "toxin detectors" and "toxin healers" are a powerful source of detoxification. (Frost 2003)

Toxin 5.14   Explosive, disruptive, condescending, and confrontational leadership behavior. **Detox 5.14.** Timely counseling, coaching, and dialogue with a destructive leader by toxin detectors and healers is a source of organizational detoxification. Regardless of the success of the intervention, the very act of a caring and timely response communicates emotional intelligence and the potential for healing.

Toxin 5.15   Avoidance of or failure to inquire into unusual or disturbing leadership behavior that persists. Disturbing surface behaviors (sudden acts of repeated narcissism, radical changes in physical appearance, multiple plastic surgeries, drastic changes in social life) may be symptomatic of serious underlying psychological issues requiring assessment and treatment. **Detox 5.15.** Timely inquiry into and response to strange or disturbing behavior may serve organizational detoxification.

Toxin 5.16 Major potentially disruptive or disturbing decisions by a leader who has exhibited strange and destructive workplace behavior. **Detox 5.16.** Under the guidance of a coach and/or management consultant the destructive leader works toward detoxification by refraining from major decision-making until he has successfully overcome the disturbing behavior. During coaching and therapy, detox is served by designating qualified alternates to publicly decide on such issues as dismissals and professional transfers.

Toxin 5.17 An organization that cannot distinguish between "healthy" and "destructive" narcissism in its leaders. (Maccoby 2007) **Detox 5.17.** In-house psychological expertise incorporating a basic DSM IV-TR knowledge to make diagnoses of mental disturbances is a powerful form of organizational protection against potentially destructive employees.

Toxin 5.18 A confrontational and hostile response by the client to an external consultant's findings and recommendations. **Detox 5.18.** Readiness to consider a contracted consultant's assessment and recommendations is a prerequisite for a healthy client-expert relationship.

Toxin 5.19 Abrupt termination of a consultation by the client who disagrees with the findings and recommendations provided by the consultants. **Detox 5.19.** An external consultant's recommendations should be thoroughly discussed, debated, and negotiated, not dismissed out of hand.

Toxin 5.20 A hostile, combative, and dysfunctional corporate environment that is carried over into the consulting relationship. **Detox 5.20.** Client and consultant should strive to make their relationship a client-centered collaboration.

Toxin 5.21 Inadequate training of new employees and neglect of continuous training regimens. **Detox 5.21.** Training of new and continuing employees should be ongoing and updated as necessary.

Toxin 5.22 Attempts to force an emotionally stretched and psychologically troubled leader to make rapid behavioral or procedural changes. **Detox 5.22.** Well-considered longer-term solutions are required if the organization believes in and wishes to retain the leader.

Toxin 5.23   Disciplining, reprimanding, transferring, demoting, or dismissing a highly valued leader who is going through psychologically trying times. **Detox 5.23.** One innovative means of demonstrating long-term commitment to a struggling leader is the creation of a "leader partnership" that gives him or her time for counseling and/or retraining.

THE DETOXIFICATION PROCESS

The detoxification of leaders and organizations is a complex process that calls for coaches and consultants who are able to identify the multiple sources and players that contribute to toxicity within a system. Organizations should exercise patience and caution in the face of toxicity; they should refrain from "jumping at the bait" and attributing the cause of dysfunctional behavior to a single event or person. Although a troubled or disruptive leader may wield an extraordinary amount of toxic influence, the detoxification process can uncover multiple and interdependent sources. Even the most poisonous acts perpetuated by a demagogue leading a massive and abrupt downsizing may be symptomatic of orders dispatched from the top of the hierarchy. Bentley Pacific's Cal Burton and Jarling-Weber's Max Lunger were just the visible talking heads representing plans and pathological agendas dictated by their companies' presidents and executive boards. Yes, Burton, Lunger, and the infamous leaders of Enron, Arthur Andersen, and other Fortune 500s are responsible for their behavior, but the nexus of the toxicity extends beyond a single head.

The sources of toxicity are not always obvious. Blaming the most visible causes and perpetrators and responding slowly to dysfunctional behavior are ways to accelerate toxicity and make it extremely difficult to address internally. The shock and dismay expressed by clients who identify their organizational pain as "already reaching into the lymph nodes" of their operations is testimony to the need for a detoxification process that incorporates affective coaching and consultation. External eyes, systemic interpretations, and innovative interventions are frequently required to detoxify work forces, grievances and lawsuits, customer relations, and corporate image.

7 Transforming Toxicity into Opportunity: From Deficits to Abundance

Changing organizations is a difficult and complicated task and large scale transformational changes are especially intractable. Between half and eighty percent of organizational change efforts fail—ranging from relatively simple adjustments, such as a new performance appraisal system or relocating personnel, or to more complicated changes such as downsizing, mergers or acquisitions, or adopting a new competitive strategy.

—K. Cameron and M. Lavine, *Making the Impossible Possible*

As a coach and consultant I have been able to move toxic leaders and organizations through assessment and detoxification. The more successful consultations result in collaborations that stimulate positive transformation of both leader and company. I begin this chapter by examining some of the deficits and negative organizational behaviors that must be overcome by toxic clients in order to reach a state of readiness for positive transformation. Numerous roadblocks, rationalizations, pseudo-interventions, ulterior motives, acts of sabotage and resistance, and the ever-present threat of irrelevant and toxic consultations can undermine the best of intentions. In the second portion of the chapter I shift from deficits and obstacles to positive organizational behaviors and the prospects for extraordinary organizational performance through an "abundance" approach to leadership (see Cameron and Lavine 2006; also see glossary).

Central to positive transformation is the contention that organizational pain and suffering can be an impetus for more than a mere return to normal functionality. The guided, informed, and trained leader is prepared to transform the extreme lessons of trauma, despair, crisis, and corporate agony into abundance leadership and superior performance. The coach, the consultant, and the client organization are collectively engaged in a move from deficits to abundance. In this chapter I illustrate the rules of transformational engagement through immersion in the second (intervention and transformation) phase of a consultation with Eisenhower Heart Institute (Chapter 3 described phase one). After detecting high levels of leadership and organizational toxicity within the institution, I recommended a strategic series of interventions. This consultation is offered as a prototype for how opportunities can be gleaned from toxicity and how deficits can trigger innovative interventions.

Let us first examine the challenge of assessing and overcoming deficits and roadblocks to positive transformation.

ASSESSING DEFICITS

Organizations suffering from high levels of toxicity are immersed in systems of deficit thinking and behavior that affects leadership, human capital, operations, and policies. As illustrated by the cases of Bentley Pacific, SkyWaves Aerospace, Eisenhower Heart Institute, Jarling-Weber Inc., and EuroText International, when deficit systems engulf the workplace, negative organizational behavior becomes the rule. A myriad of dysfunctions affect relations between leaders and subordinates, research and development, work teams, and customer service; the result is a toxic system. In working with clients I have found that developing a comprehensive approach to deficits and negative organizational behavior is a prerequisite to finding insight and moving toward a more functional and finally a superior state. In this chapter I address organizations and leadership along a continuum from the highly dysfunctional and toxic, to functional behavior and operations, to superior performance and abundance leadership (see Figure 2 in the Introduction).

Demagoguery, prolonged conflict, sabotage, the abrupt hiring of mercenary CEOs, and savage overnight restructurings constitute extreme deficits and are on the short list of prime sources of toxicity in organizations. Although the toxic leader is typically positioned at the epicenter of a firm's upheaval, it should also be apparent that it takes more than a single Al "Chainsaw" Dunlap to wreak havoc at Scott Paper or Sunbeam. Why? Toxic leaders operate primarily within malleable or hospitable organizational cultures. The slash-and-burn management style of Dunlap was once celebrated in Fortune 500 circles and the media, and it influenced the cost-containment strategy of many organizations (including Bentley Pacific's Cal Burton and Jarling-Weber's Max Lunger as discussed in Chapters 1 and 4 of this book). Both leaders operated in close tandem with their executive boards and top-tier leadership. Once coaches, consultants, and analysts had systematically probed the deficit strategies and carnage of these companies, they recognized that the "fish rots from the head down" logic would only take them so far. Although the companies' leaders did at times victimize and blindside their employees and constituents, another side of the story reveals an insidious camaraderie between the toxic CEOs, their executive boards, and upper echelon leadership.

One obvious question relates to the hiring of a toxic leader in the first place. Why did Scott Paper and Sunbeam hire Al "Chainsaw" Dunlap? Why did Bentley Pacific hire Cal Burton? Why did Jarling-Weber hire Max Lunger? Once you realize that the recruiters, human resources, and selection committees were just complying with the opportunistic soldier-of-fortune agendas of their boards and superiors, you are ready to play on the next level of the toxicity game. There is no quick and easy way to exorcise a leader or to make a precise incision that eliminates the nexus of a corporate cancer. In fact, it is quite probable that the removal of a toxic leader will leave behind a highly destructive culture largely unscathed and awaiting the arrival of the next toxic leader. Dirty corporate waters sometimes run very deep.

At best, the rapid removal of a toxic leader as a driving figurehead and symptom of systemwide dysfunction will bring a temporary sigh of relief and sense of renewal, and the illusion that significant organizational change is about to happen. But in the bright lights and big city of Fortune 500 companies, firing the leader may in fact be a cheap and deceptive shot. It's an exercise in knocking off one of the serpent's heads while the creature is already busy growing five more. No one should be surprised when a new "toxin-free" leader soon becomes immersed in another round of companywide dysfunction. Despite a change in leadership, the problems remain. Toxicity prevails because it is entrenched in the system.

The purpose of detoxification is to transform dysfunctional policies, operations, and leaders into more functional ones. This process involves evaluating and following the trail of toxicity throughout an organization. Unfortunately, some coaches and consultants, in part owing to their limited expertise and insight, will lead you down the path of treating only the symptoms of toxicity (see Bradford and Burke 2005a). Worse, they will add insult to injury by delivering expensive consulting reports and claiming that they are based on the extensive evidence they uncovered (Schaffer 2002). In my role as leadership coach and consultant, I thoroughly enjoy introducing the concept of detoxification to clients. It takes only a moment or two to assure the client that detoxification does not necessarily involve a twelve-step program such as those used to break addiction to alcohol or cocaine. But it's still a good analogy. My goal is to sober up an inebriated organization by changing its destructive behavior.

The doctor-patient analogy also applies to identifying core issues in coach and client relationships. The best coaches and consultants perform the equivalent of a differential diagnosis, searching for toxins throughout an organization much as a doctor conducts a comprehensive checkup of her patient or the psychiatrist collaborates with the neurologist in evaluating a brain scan. Once deficits and trouble spots are located and sources of toxicity are pinpointed, it is critical to connect the dots.

As we witnessed in the Eisenhower Heart Institute case, Dr. Lorimer was initially thought to be the guilty party. But the hotheaded, aggressive, in-your-face heart surgeon was hardly one-dimensional; nor was his hospital. As a highly trained and renowned mitral valve specialist, he would be the first to testify that he spent most of his time honing his technical surgical skills. Social intelligence and emotional competency with nurses, surgical assistants, staff, and patients were an afterthought. Dr. Lorimer did not give much thought to his bedside manner or to the communication skills he employed when meeting with patients and their families before surgery. Not surprisingly, when a surgery went wrong, the lack of dialogue and relationship building with the patient's family would come back to haunt him and subsequently implicate the anesthesiologist and everyone who was involved in the treatment of the patient. It was guilt by association. But despite Dr. Lorimer's deficits of emotional and social intelligence, the brilliant heart surgeon was not viewed by external consultants or his clinical coach as the lone toxic party in the Eisenhower debacle. Closer assessment by the external coach revealed the less visible side of the toxic terrain surrounding Dr. Lorimer. There was much comparative negligence located in the human resources department and the employee assistance program, as well as among the internal and externally contracted training and development specialists, the executive leadership, and upper echelon decision-makers who sent the organization into a tailspin with a poorly conceived restructuring. The hospital's executive board, CEO, president, HR director, and cardiac surgeons and nurses attempted to point the finger at Dr. Lorimer as the loose cannon with an anger management problem, but the toxicity was far more widespread. The straightforward case of the allegedly toxic surgeon soon revealed the need to detoxify corporate strategy, decision-makers, and operations within the organization.

FROM DETOXIFICATION TO TRANSFORMATION

Recognizing the need for detoxification sets the stage for organizational upheaval, change, reflection, and potential transformation. Opportunity abounds. Avoidance and denial are no longer options. Probing consultations with clients in advanced stages of dysfunction and toxicity suggest critical questions. The questions that Eisenhower Heart Institute needed to answer before beginning the second phase of coaching were:

- Is our leader, Dr. Lorimer, toxic beyond repair? Is his behavior due to personal mental and emotional issues? Is his behavior pathological?
- Is our leader a candidate for detoxification, renewal, and rejuvenation?
- Is our leader operating primarily as an independently toxic agent or do his problems reflect a thoroughly toxic organizational system?
- Is this organization in a reversible or an irreversible state of entropy and decline?
- Can visionary and abundance leadership pull our organization out of the dumps and help it rise again?
- Will destructiveness and decay engulf operations, or will transformational leadership rise to the occasion?
- In the face of toxicity is it still possible to celebrate our organization's strengths?
- How can we alter the collective language and mindset from deficits to assets?
- How does our organization transform poor performance into superior performance?
- How does our organization move from deficit thinking into abundance thinking?
- How does our organization move from a focus on negative deviance to a prioritizing of positive deviance?
- Can we locate a prototype of a leader able to transform toxicity into opportunity, superior performance, and abundance?

As a leadership coach I am quick to testify that a diagnosis of toxicity provokes and upsets the status quo. There are many deficits, destructive tendencies, and threats to assess and overcome. Upper echelon leaders turn to their coaches and consultants. As illustrated throughout this book, the external coach is frequently called upon too late in the game. The early bird is at a distinct advantage. Detoxification and positive transformation are infinitely more possible if the cavalry is summoned before the villagers are slaughtered and all hope is lost. When organizations delay action until they are faced with workplace deaths, violence, grievances, and litigation, the damage is difficult to reverse. How do leaders respond to serious adversity? Once forced to publicly acknowledge a problem and take action, their natural inclination is to finance a fact-finding mission in a misguided belief that the "data will solve all." Beware of the consultant who seeks only "hard evidence."

It is not uncommon for leaders to be almost frantic in their response to crisis situations. Toxicity breeds fear in the workplace, adversely affects customer and patient services, and may even undermine working relationships with contracted external experts. And fearful leaders unwittingly extend their toxicity into relationships with coaches and consultants. A coach uses his experience and insight to calm such clients. The ability to conduct respectful dialogue and build trust is critical. Frank discussions can begin to turn subtext into text and render the invisible visible. Behavioral change requires that consultants get immersed, stay involved, and overcome the all-to-common implementation vacuum.

ROADBLOCKS TO TRANSFORMATION

There are many roadblocks on the road to positive transformation. Through the consultations described in this book I have attempted to describe the steps in a firm's transformation from toxicity to detoxification and back to health. The seeds of transformation are sown when coach and client are able to sufficiently trust, empathize, and collaborate en route to generating interventions that break through some of the prototypical toxic patterns and resistances (e.g., see Bateson 1969, 1972; Watzlawick, Beavin, and Jackson 1967); Wilder and Collins 1994).

A recurring recipe for failure in coaching and consultation is the client's insistence that a needs assessment is unnecessary and unwarranted. Recall from Chapter 5 that the executive board of EuroText's Brussels headquarters mandated that their consultants find what they had already found and rubber stamp the company's own toxic diagnosis. Similarly, the leadership of Jarling-Weber expected the external experts to concur with the client firm's predetermined assessments of their problems. That ethical stalemate was eventually broken by the external experts' use of the Harvard Negotiation Project's world-class negotiation and conflict resolution techniques. Finally, and innovatively, a clinical coach became a personal confidant and therapist to the troubled leader at the center of the EuroText storm. The resulting transformation included a groundbreaking restructuring of leadership with a shift from single to dual leadership. So much for the single heroic leader.

Other roadblocks to organizational and leader transformation presented themselves at SkyWaves Aerospace (Chapter 2) when "rogue" engineers threatened to post injurious comments about their company on the Internet. The low-profile CEO at SkyWaves ordered the consultants to "nip this employee sabotage in the bud," an assignment not easily fulfilled. Initially, the SkyWaves leaders had little interest in assessing the origins or underlying causes of the dispute. Dialogue was not even considered. The prospect of open communication was blocked at every juncture. The leaders wanted the consultants to buy into a win-lose game plan whereby the offending employees would be reprimanded or dismissed. This part of the client's agenda was one-dimensional—it was punitive and toxic. The skill of the consultants redirected the conversation to more productive issues.

TOXIC CLIENTS

Toxic clients are common (see Schein 2005). A leading U.S. kitchen appliance company, for example, attempted to manipulate a consulting team into utilizing 360-degree feedback to generate bogus, self-serving data that would incriminate and publicly demean a targeted executive. The client whispered, "Let's orchestrate this so it's an evidence-based firing. The facts don't lie. And you'll get us the facts that we need. Right coach?" In the toxic world of my clients, evidence is approached most honestly through extensive direct observation in the context of their day-to-day workplace. Understanding an organizational context requires field study, description, and narrative. I believe that the term "business anthropology" is appropriate. Too many clients and consultants are in a crazy hurry to generate data rather than to soberly assess complex toxic behavior and culture. Superficial soundbite approaches to consultations don't work.

On the road toward reflection and self-examination both coach and client must avoid stepping on some common land mines:

- Refrain from manipulating data or being bamboozled by manipulated data.
- Avoid quick and easy solutions to complex problems.
- Refrain from buying into one-dimensional bean counting for the sake of quantification (see Rosenzweig 2007).

- Be wary of simplistic views of causality.
- Do not give in to a client's desire to collect data that proves what they want it to prove (Rosenzweig 2004).

When the client organization calls for a coach or consultant, it is a time for pondering and truth-seeking, not quick fixes. Toxicity should summon deep and resourceful self-examination. The foundation of the business—its vision, culture, ambiance, and approach to communicating with subordinates and between constituencies—requires transparency. Clear-minded detoxification and organizational housecleaning are in order. As a consultant and coach I train organizations to engage in what Argyris (2004) termed double-loop learning. This process requires a probing of typically unexamined and taken-for-granted corporate axioms and postulates that underlie the operations of everyday business life. Toxicity provides astute coaches and leaders with opportunities to go back to the drawing board, embrace a comprehensive detoxification process, and move forward toward renewal and revitalization.

TRANSFORMING TOXICITY INTO OPPORTUNITY

By the time human resources, executive board members, presidents, and CEOs apply the label "toxic" to their firm, conflicts and dysfunctions may well have metastasized throughout the organization and fear and urgency set in. In responding to high levels of toxicity with a ninth-inning call to an external coach, the organization finally acknowledges the need for help and adopts a mindset that is potentially ripe for transformation.

Trauma opens doors (Tedeschi, Park, and Calhoun 1998). Disagreements can cause leaders to engage in sorely needed and overdue dialogue. When demagogues push too hard, the workforce finds a voice and a stage for empowerment. Victims of downsizings question the wisdom of drastic cost-containment measures. In contrast, a necessary downsizing that treats employees well provides opportunities. At North Country Solutions in Vancouver, the firm's CEO benchmarked a better way to simultaneously terminate and care about dismissed employees and build up psychological capital with those who were retained (see Luthans, Youssef, and Avolio 2007a, 2007b). And a brilliant but emotionally incompetent surgeon, Dr. Ivan Lorimer, nevertheless provided potential leadership and a capacity for superior performance that was central to a remarkable transformation at Eisenhower Heart Institute.

Any transformation begins with a change in thinking and vocabulary. As the coach or consultant I am told about disasters, tragedies, mishaps, traumas, conflicts, and deficits. I listen carefully to my clients in order to recognize the roadblocks and obstacles to readiness. I look for an opening to turn the corner from negative to positive. Rather than dwelling on what went wrong, I try to re-direct their attention to what has worked and how to build on those successes. A positive approach to change challenges the organization and leadership and ultimately replaces a motivation based on fear with a vision based on abundance.

TRANSFORMATION AT EISENHOWER HEART INSTITUTE

As the coach who belatedly entered into this highly toxic organization, I perceived both Dr. Lorimer and Eisenhower Heart Institute as standing at a developmental crossroads at the end of the first phase of the consultation. Interventions were introduced to alleviate the stress level, anger, and anxiety of Dr. Lorimer and his colleagues, to lower organizational toxicity levels, to alleviate grievances and internal conflicts, and to better anticipate and lower the probabilities of surgical mishaps and medical malpractice claims.

The thrust of the first phase of the consultation was to move leadership, the cardiology division, and the entire organizational system out of high toxicity and into a more functional state of operations. Every effort was made to reduce conflict during open-heart surgeries and also during cardiology roundtable meetings. A modest level of stability and normalization was eventually reached at Eisenhower Heart Institute by the end of the first phase of the consultation.

After that early progress, the client requested that I enter into a second consultation phase in order to address the longer-term issues, vision, and questions surrounding the organization's leadership. The leaders were most concerned about the prospects for "gaining momentum as a center of excellence" and moving their cardiology division "to the next level." They requested that I work primarily with Dr. Lorimer because he was viewed as the key to further developing the hospital's role in performing the innovative mitral valve repair technique. Although some issues and differences remained between the CEO, Dr. Marshall Portello, and Dr. Lorimer, the powers that be were satisfied that toxicity was receding and that Eisenhower was now "focused on the big picture of becoming a world-class cardiac surgery division." Although the CEO remained skeptical of Dr. Lorimer's emotional and social competency with colleagues and patients, he had no concerns related to the surgeon's talent, credentials, and work ethic. Dr. Portello had become protective and visionary in regard to the exclusive minimal-incision mitral valve surgeries perfected at Eisenhower.

With so much riding on building up this specialization and bringing it to center stage, the hospital wanted to prevent any adverse publicity or tort claims. In our phase two contracting and articulation session, I highlighted the centrality of achieving a "zero-defects" level of postoperative patient satisfaction in cardiac surgery. There was an instant positive response from Dr. Portello. Moreover, after an exchange of e-mails Dr. Lorimer was also fully on board with the zero-defects agenda. Both were quite comfortable and actually relieved to have a few measurables and deliverables on the agenda. Dr. Lorimer in particular was enthusiastic about quantifying a zero-defects metric for his minimal-incision surgeries. I detected a new hopefulness and optimism in both Portello and Lorimer about Eisenhower's future.

TOWARD AN ABUNDANCE VISION

At the outset of the second phase of the consultation and coaching I was informed that Eisenhower's top leadership wanted to move vigorously forward in pursuit of a mission of excellence. Dr. Ivan Lorimer was at the center of this abundance vision. Leadership was acutely aware of Dr. Lorimer's worldwide prominence in his field. Dr. Portello and his associates were quite clear that as a personal coach for Dr. Lorimer and a consultant for Eisenhower-at-large I was to work on the premise that "all roads go through Dr. Lorimer." This led to the establishment of a cross-functional leadership team comprising Dr. Portello, Dr. Lorimer, and myself, because the CEO wanted to bring force and clarity to the empowerment of his surgeon. After a brainstorming session, both Dr. Portello and Dr. Lorimer accepted my idea to establish the "Mitral Valve Project" (MVP) as a means of bringing a brand name and instant identification to the visionary and innovative work of Dr. Lorimer and colleagues. We called a more technical variation of this brand the "Minimal-Incision Mitral Valve Project" (MIMVP).

In the phase two reentry and contractual talks with the CEO and colleagues I emphasized that a solo focus on Dr. Lorimer would not be optimal. This was consistent with my earlier assessment and report at the close of phase one. While Dr. Portello was attempting to simplify matters by shining the spotlight on Dr. Lorimer (and I concurred up to a point), I worked with the CEO to ensure that Dr. Lorimer was not perceived as solely responsible for the earlier toxicity and likewise would not be the single passageway to a new vision and world-class performance. Specifically, I went back over the recommendations, referring to the role of human resources, the employee assistance program, lines of communication between Dr. Lorimer and colleagues, nurses, staff and upper management, and other interrelated players in the Eisenhower system. Of particular concern was the need to revisit and rearticulate Dr. Lorimer's role as the chair of the cardiology division, the parameters of his leadership, and the impact of the recent and troubling restructuring.

Dr. Portello extended carte blanche to me to make a second round of recommendations and strategize systemwide interventions—all in support of Dr. Lorimer as the centerpiece and driving engine. (I was able to live with Dr. Lorimer as the central player or nexus in a transformational Eisenhower system.) One remaining concern surrounded the questionable restructuring that Eisenhower had undertaken via the Durk and Borgus Consulting Group. Dr. Portello had taken my earlier assessment to heart and agreed that the restructuring had been too much, too soon. The restructuring needed to be revisited, in part because it was undermining the authority of Dr. Lorimer, as well as creating confusion and what I called a "horizontal tyranny and leaderless disrespect." Part of the agreement with Dr. Portello and the executive board entailed addressing the implementation gap or vortex created by the hit-and-run restructuring by establishing a companywide commitment to continuous improvement. This would be achieved in part through individual and team coaching, and through training and development to install the new management philosophy that had been introduced only marginally by Durk and Borgus. Dr. Portello did not want a second round of Durk and Borgus and appreciated that I had been part of the "cleanup crew" after the disruptive and ill-conceived restructuring and training regimen.

COACHING TO WORK THROUGH DEFICITS

In the second phase of coaching with Dr. Lorimer I was allowed to reveal the intentions of upper echelon management, including those of the surgeon's former adversary, Dr. Portello. Dr. Lorimer was pleased to learn of his support upstairs, but he remained cautious and skeptical of his chances for survival and his ability to excel at Eisenhower. He feared the damage done by the fly-by-night restructuring; he questioned the chances of restoring good relations with his surgical team and regaining the support of hospital executives. He unloaded a cart of questions directed at me: Why the turnaround upstairs? Did phase one of the coaching and consultation change Dr. Portello's attitude toward me from the toxic and guilty surgeon to the newly endowed hero of positive transformational change? What was behind all of this? I assured Dr. Lorimer that Dr. Portello himself had stated that "all roads go through Dr. Lorimer."

It was a bit troubling to learn, however, that Lorimer had never expected this turnaround. Expecting the worst or more of the same, Dr. Lorimer revealed to me that he had been "secretly investigating options at other institutions." As one of five prodigies of Dr. Antonin Breton, the originator of the noninvasive mitral valve repair procedure, Ivan Lorimer felt deeply that he was on a mission to make "major breakthroughs in heart surgery." In a nutshell, he had not bargained for the hostility, extreme conflict, and agitation that engulfed him at Eisenhower Heart Institute. He observed, "I am hardly an angel, but I am a masterful surgeon who doesn't spend too much time concentrating on social etiquette with subordinates and colleagues. I am about surgery and perfection to the nth degree." More than willing to acknowledge that he had been explosive, hotheaded, loud, condescending, and abrasive both at the surgical table and in team roundtables, Dr. Lorimer confessed, "I just want to get on with my work. I am not a communicator, a socially intelligent dude, or remotely interested in good vibrations and fulfilling communication. I just want to perfect these procedures and get as close to zero defects as is humanly possible."

Our dialogues revealed the doctor's extreme devotion to carrying the torch of his mentor and his dedication to perfection. Clearly his views were consistent with the postulates and axioms underlying both total quality management and Six Sigma (see glossary). As Dr. Lorimer saw it, the world-class quality that he envisioned providing was "jeopardized every time I enter surgery due to the lower levels of competency and technical awareness of my surgical teams." It was hardly a stretch to understand his stress and agitation when he was faced with members of surgical teams who in his words were "amateurish and embarrassing."

Although Dr. Lorimer was an analytical and detail-oriented specialist, he was also quite emotional, but with an emphasis on the darker end of the emotional continuum. He was extremely graphic when it came to expressing displeasure, letdowns, and acts of incompetence, but sorely lacking in expressing warmth, support, or empathy and in the interpersonal skills useful for operating in a high-stress workplace.

A transition had to be made, however, if cardiac surgery at Eisenhower was to become the center for excellence that Dr. Lorimer and the hospital aspired to. As Lorimer's leadership coach I felt it was time to shift the rhetoric from negative to positive and from deficit to abundance. Initially, Dr. Lorimer was my primary vehicle for instigating positive transformation at the hospital. With the blessings of the CEO and his entourage I was able to continue functioning as a coach and consultant-without-boundaries. Dr. Lorimer was aware of this agreement with Dr. Portello and he was fully on board.

Dr. Lorimer caught on quickly and responded well. Trustworthiness, collaboration, and authenticity were the qualities that opened up the surgeon. There was much on his mind. As a complex and intelligent man he was more than ready to be mentally and emotionally probed. In the metaphorical sense I was conducting an exploratory cognitive and affective examination of Dr. Lorimer's motives and visions for his professional life.

I explained the new positive organizational behavior ground rules to the doctor during our third session in the second phase of the consultation. My mission was to build up psychological capital (see Luthans, Avolio, Walumbwa, and Li 2005; Luthans, Youssef, and Avolio 2007a, 2007b) through:

a. optimism (see Scheier and Carver 1985; Segestrom, Taylor, Kemeny, and Fahey 1998; Seligman 1998);

b. hope (McDermott and Snyder 1999; Michael 2000; Snyder et al. 1991); and

c. resilience (Block and Kremen 1996; Masten 2001; Masten and Reed 2002).

The goal of transformation to positive language, thoughts, emotions, behavior, and leadership was front and center. I highlighted the positive agenda with Dr. Lorimer in simple, everyday language: "Positive. Positive. Positive. We've established you are world class in your mitral valve repair work. The executive wants to back you to the ends of the earth—if we can connect the dots. Let's see where the gaps are—our abundance gaps. It's time for the rubber to hit the road."

During one session Dr. Lorimer told me that he missed his friends from Paris. He was referring to the small inner circle of young surgeons who had studied under Dr. Breton. In particular, he said, there was one colleague that he considered "my brother and my other half." He was referring to an Israeli surgeon, Dr. Avi Zaroff, who was currently practicing at a center for excellence in Houston, Texas. Lorimer told me that he had recently contacted Zaroff to see whether his friend knew of any prospects. To Lorimer's surprise he discovered that Zaroff had encountered similar issues at his institution and was secretly on the job market himself. Their communication had ceased about three months earlier when busy schedules intervened.

During the same coaching session Dr. Lorimer talked about "the burden of being the single heroic leader." Although he was pleased to be out of the doghouse and finally appreciated by executives, he still had serious reservations about his role at Eisenhower. Exploring this, I found that although he wanted to "dramatically change the course of mitral valve procedures around the world and carry the torch of Dr. Breton," he was nevertheless not at all interested in being a center of attention. Dr. Lorimer just wanted to get on with his work.

Dr. Lorimer's homework was to get back in touch with Dr. Zaroff. It went exactly as I hoped it would. At the next session he asked, "How do you think the executives would feel about rightsizing cardiology?" I told him that they were willing to consider anything. Lorimer's "dream scenario" was right in line with what I had been thinking. He wanted to know whether the time might be right to run a "strategic hire" by Dr. Portello. Lorimer's buddy Zaroff was at his wit's end in Houston and the two doctors had discussed the prospect of a partnership or dual leadership at Eisenhower. Lorimer explained that if he could get Dr. Zaroff to join him it would be a coup on multiple levels:

1. Eisenhower would have two out of five of Dr. Breton's protégées—a singular feat in the world of cardiology.

2. The two were fast friends and had worked together seamlessly in Paris. They were a proven commodity and team.

3. Zaroff possessed not only the obsession for perfection but also a "right-brain, intuitive, and magical ability to communicate with patients and colleagues." Dr. Lorimer testified that Dr. Zaroff would supply all the communication, emotional intelligence, and social intelligence pieces that were missing from his own game.

4. Lorimer offered that Zaroff was perhaps the only one who could "make nice" with Nurse Gleesom, his surgical team, and his agitated brethren in cardiology.

5. Dr. Zaroff was in Dr. Lorimer's view the "archangel" who would be able to pick up the pieces of several lingering grievances filed by former surgical patients who were displeased with their results. Zaroff's extraordinary social skills, Lorimer believed, would make him the perfect negotiator and arbitrator on behalf of himself and the institution. The goal was to wipe the slate clean and have no questions hovering over the credibility of the minimally invasive mitral valve project.

By the time Lorimer was through, he had compiled a fourteen-point list of the virtues of a dual leadership format—pending the hire of Dr. Avi Zaroff. It was an impressive breakthrough en route to abundance leadership.

FROM SINGLE DEFICIT TO DUAL ABUNDANCE LEADERSHIP

For the first time, Dr. Lorimer became truly animated and viscerally expressive. The prospect of bringing his Israeli colleague on board in a leadership role beside him was riveting. I completely concurred. I had had to muzzle myself a week earlier not to make the same suggestion myself, but hoped that something very constructive might emerge when Dr. Lorimer reestablished contact with Dr. Zaroff.

I worked swiftly. I had Dr. Lorimer download a vita and a wealth of material on Dr. Zaroff and the pitch was made to Dr. Portello. The CEO was intrigued on two major fronts. First, the fact that Eisenhower would be the home to 40 percent, or two out of the five of the master surgeons from Dr. Breton's stable was enticing. Second, Portello was eager to remove some of the spotlight from Dr. Lorimer.

Within ten days Dr. Zaroff arrived for extensive rounds of interviews. Zaroff was a huge hit, and the Eisenhower executives did their best to meet his needs before his home hospital made a more attractive counteroffer. Over a period of three weeks the hire was finalized. In the restructured cardiology division Dr. Zaroff took over as the leader of the "roundtable" meetings, and many of the interpersonal and people problems dissipated. Dr. Lorimer took leadership of a new "continuous improvement" program featuring training and development on mitral valve repair. In partnership, the two developed a program stressing transparency during selected surgeries; open-heart procedures became tutorials and learning venues for other surgeons, nurses, and staff who lacked experience in the minimally invasive techniques. Through the reunion the two surgeons reconstructed a piece of their Paris relationship at the Eisenhower Heart Institute. Where an organization and a cardiology division had been in decline, new life emerged. Desperation, deficits, and anger were transformed into enthusiasm and hope. A brittle, defeatist attitude was overtaken by resilience and renewal. The cardiology division was given a new life and future with the hospital's complete support.

Dr. Lorimer and I agreed to incorporate the recently arrived Dr. Zaroff into some of our coaching sessions. At Zaroff's first session with us I distinctly recall saying to the two surgeons that in most organizations a single leader cannot produce extraordinary success (Cameron and Lavine 2006, p. 227). Dr. Lorimer was quick to add that "now we have a prototype for multiple leaders. Do we not?" He was quite correct. Not only had we established dual leadership in cardiology, we were also paving the way by example for multiple leadership and cross-fertilization throughout the institution. It had already been hypothesized that a new flatter organization would move away from the top-down, single-leadership model and develop horizontal rule by multiple leaders. This was well under way in cardiology.

Under the dual leadership agenda and related and emerging innovations in cardiology, productivity was up and the numbers looked promising. Internal and customer grievances plunged within eleven weeks after the arrival of Dr. Zaroff, and this success was accompanied by an unprecedented 99.4 percent success rate in mitral valve surgeries, at least several percentage points higher than the top three competing centers for excellence. Profits soared. Stakeholders were charmed. The Zaroff and Lorimer duo was just what the doctor ordered.

PATIENT EDUCATION AND TRAINING

The only grievances still occasionally surfacing were from patients and families who were disappointed when the mitral valve repair procedure was aborted during mid-surgery by either Dr. Lorimer or Dr. Zaroff. This late decision was always due to patient complications and risk factors. In these few cases the doctor implanted a mechanical valve or a pig valve instead of attempting an overly dangerous repair.

The complaints or "failures" were given the highest priority since bad press or medical malpractice litigation always loomed as a threat. Even in the case of a frivolous case without merit, publicity could be damaging to the groundbreaking and visionary agenda of the mitral valve team. Thus when two dissatisfied patients filed reports and hinted at litigation, this led to a roundtable airing of the grievances and a new intervention partially initiated and backed by the leadership coach. I suggested that a supercharged 360-degree effort to educate and inform patients and families before surgery could alleviate much of their disappointment. In addition, I stressed that these incidents represented "abundance gaps," not failures or deficits. I reiterated repeatedly, as if it were a mantra, "We are no longer caught up in that old-world game of what went wrong." I explained that although the hospital's mitral valve repair program had been spectacularly successful, there were always going to be patients who required another route or an alternative procedure. These situations presented additional options, not obstacles.

In an effort to build bridges through dialogue, our collaborations in training and development initially included Dr. Lorimer, Dr. Zaroff, five cardiologists, two junior cardiac surgeons, and a supporting cast of seven nurses, assorted technicians, and two observer-only members of HR. All of these participants (excluding HR) had observed Dr. Zaroff and Dr. Lorimer's surgeries, had attended multiple tutorials, and had a fairly extensive knowledge of the extraordinary advantages provided to the patient by the mitral valve procedures at Eisenhower. The training regimen grew to further include anesthesiologists and all postoperative cardiologists, nurses, and staff who served patients in the week or more following open-heart surgery.

Not only did this program achieve the intended outcomes (zero patient grievances within three months of initiation of the program), but it was also quite useful in addressing outside-the-box and unanticipated patient issues. The typical patient complaint was having to live with a mechanical valve accompanied by a lifelong prescription for blood thinner. Expecting a repair but receiving a mechanical valve, some patients immediately thought "grievance and litigation," and every now and then there was a grievance or a patient conflict, or a threat. *But, consistent with transformation, every potentially toxic threat was to be rerouted as an opportunity and treated as an abundance gap.* One patient's story is particularly memorable.

THE TOXIC PIG VALVE: SEIZING OPPORTUNITY FROM TOXICITY

An orthodox Jewish patient became almost hysterical when he learned postoperatively that during the procedure Dr. Zaroff and Dr. Lorimer had jointly concluded that a repair was not recommended in his case. The patient, Shane Shapiro, would have been at risk, and in the surgeons' judgment a repair would have had a high risk of failure. Dr. Zaroff and Dr. Lorimer opted instead to insert a pig valve. The kicker was that the patient, an orthodox, religious Jew, was distressed that "a non-Kosher, heathen animal part" had been "implanted within the heart and soul of my body." Although he claimed to fully understand that the pig valve was in the surgeons' view the best choice and offered more longevity and safety in his case than the dangers inherent in a repair, he and his wife were considering a possible medical malpractice claim. This upsetting and toxic prospect required reflection. Rather than see this unusual conflict escalate into a toxic public relations spectacle and a damaging courtroom debacle, it was crucial to call the principles of abundance leadership into play.

Dr. Lorimer, Dr. Zaroff, the HR director, Dr. Portello, and I convened an emergency "Patient Excellence" meeting. Our broad objective was to use this opportunity to build solidarity and, to my way of thinking, operationalize the cross fertilization of leaders in dealing with a very real patient issue. Recognizing that this potential meltdown had Biblical, Talmudic, and Old Testament subtext lurking, I had a brainstorm. I proposed to the group that I contact a close friend, a rabbi who was the leader of a conservative Jewish synagogue. Rabbi Lew Reisman had been trained as an orthodox rabbi but chose to practice as a middle-of-the-road conservative. The rabbi had the highest level of traditional orthodox training and also was steeped in secular society. In addition, the rabbi was a state-licensed social worker and professionally licensed counselor and a superb communicator, mediator, and conflict resolution professional. Eisenhower's HR asked the rabbi to intervene in the Shapiro case in the role of a psychotherapist and external consultant.

What occurred between Rabbi Reisman and Mr. Shapiro was a truly remarkable lesson in how organizations can be innovative and create opportunity out of potentially toxic situations. Mr. Shapiro's jaw dropped when he was presented with the option of consulting with Rabbi Reisman. He buoyantly accepted. The initial fifteen minutes of the first session was cool and reserved, but soon morphed into a biblical and Talmudic dialogue that addressed the issue of the pig valve in Mr. Shapiro's heart from no fewer than fifteen perspectives, all grounded in scripture. The exchange that ensued over three consulting and coaching sessions went beyond the scope of talented screenwriters. Following three "exploratory dialogue sessions" the Eisenhower leadership team was granted permission by the rabbi and Mr. Shapiro to attend the formal arbitration scenario. Although it would take many pages to decode and decipher the life lessons contained in this remarkable interaction, suffice it to say that a developmental and training tutorial unfolded at Eisenhower that may soon serve as a tutorial for management consultants and client organizations. Shapiro dropped his grievance and withdrew his threats of malpractice against the cardiac surgeons and the hospital. The potentially toxic postoperative patient became a major financial contributor to the Eisenhower Mitral Valve Project. Shapiro was transformed into a one-man dream PR team. His extraordinary support extended into the community in the form of speeches singing the praises of the mitral valve surgeons at Eisenhower.

Finally, in the spirit of 360-degree abundance leadership, the hospital offered Rabbi Reisman a contract as a patient-counselor and religious and spiritual adviser to heart surgery patients and their families. Although the chances of a repeat of the Shapiro case were infinitesimal, there was an ongoing need to prepare patients for life-threatening surgery by addressing their fears, emotions, and thoughts about mortality and death, and through counseling about optimism and transformation to a postoperative "healthy heart" existence. Rabbi Reisman was extremely successful in closing some of the abundance gaps in emotional and social intelligence and competence at the hospital. When the media found out about Eisenhower's rabbinical counseling and got wind of the Shapiro "pig valve case," their coverage raised international awareness of the innovation and excellence of the Mitral Valve Project.

SUMMARY

Recognizing and seizing the opportunities to transform toxicity can be a turning point for an organization. At Eisenhower, rather than continuing to single out one leader as the source of the escalating organizational conflict, the leadership was willing to entertain the alternative assessment of the coach and consultant. Rather than degrade the social skills of Dr. Lorimer, the consultant recommended that his strengths be stressed. Dr. Lorimer was only one of five doctors trained in a world-renowned minimally invasive heart surgery procedure. Taking the abundance approach, the hospital's leadership developed a new vision statement and mission around the unique talents of Dr. Lorimer. The new Mitral Valve Project symbolized an institutionalizing of and a commitment to transformational organizational change.

The central vision was refined with the hiring of Dr. Lorimer's colleague from Paris, Dr. Zaroff. Critical was the ability of Eisenhower Heart Institute to move toward dual leadership by the technically expert Dr. Lorimer and the socially and technically skilled Dr. Zaroff. Together they set the tone for institute-wide coordination between divisions and areas of expertise with an aggressive pursuit of congruence and alignment between administrators, orderlies, nurses, doctors, surgeons, and a variety of specialists and support staff.

Following the lead of the consultant, upper echelon leadership pointed the way toward systemwide positive organizational behavior resulting in what Cameron and Lavine (2006) refer to as an amplifying and heliotropic effect (see Cameron, Dutton, and Quinn 2003). Much as a houseplant will bend toward the sunlight, so will the players in an organization direct their thoughts, feelings, and behaviors toward positivity and a "leadership of abundance." In response to Eisenhower's collective experiences of threat and trauma, a collective confidence or efficacy emerged as human liabilities were strategically transformed into social capital. Powerful moves toward team building, quality control, collective pursuit of zero defects, continuous improvement, and ongoing training and development all consolidated a deep commitment to human factors. Noteworthy was the opening up of previously closed doors: the heart specialists, Dr. Lorimer and Dr. Zaroff, increasingly served as mentors to nurses and cardiac surgeons and provided open-heart surgeries as a training and development venue. Moreover, the two surgeons were instrumental in establishing a "surgeon of the year award," with the winning cardiac surgeon being granted a fully funded six-month period of study in Paris with Dr. Breton. Now fully committed to a future of multiple leadership in the Mitral Valve Project, Dr. Portello expressed the intention to regularly "grow new leaders on our cardiac surgery farm in Paris."

PRINCIPLES FOR MOVING TOWARD SPECTACULAR PERFORMANCE

The breakthroughs experienced through the dual leadership of Dr. Zaroff and Dr. Lorimer continued to spawn a groundswell of innovations and transformations affecting policies, operations, and human capital issues throughout the Eisenhower Heart Institute system. In the following inventory I cite some of the more influential and transformational changes that moved the organization from deficit operations to spectacular performance. Although many of the following examples are specific to Eisenhower Heart Institute, the principles can be adapted for use by any organization committed to transforming toxicity into opportunity.

1. *Move from single to dual leadership.* A shift from a single heroic leader concept into dual and multiple leaders with multiple roles.

2. *Rightsize.* The strategic decision by a client to add or subtract leadership to create a more effective team. A strategic rightsizing decision originating with Dr. Lorimer and his personal leadership coach was sanctioned by the CEO. The rightsizing at Eisenhower added a professionally skilled and authentic leader who could strengthen and add value to Dr. Lorimer's leadership.

3. *Establish collaborative leadership.* A collaboration among leaders throughout the organization. In addition to the dual leadership in cardiology, the collaboration among representatives of the hospital's medical and administrative divisions contributed to restoring organizational health.

4. *Develop a profound organizational vision.* At Eisenhower, the "Minimal-Incision Mitral Valve Project" became the flagship project for innovation and excellence at the nexus of the hospital's new vision statement.

5. *Move from deficit to abundance thinking.* Following the new precedent established in cardiology via the team of Dr. Lorimer and Dr. Zaroff, leadership throughout the Eisenhower Heart Institute transitioned from dealing with deficit gaps and problems to closing abundance gaps when they arose.

6. *Treat obstacles as opportunities.* Eisenhower leadership transformed the organization by focusing less on obstacles and more on opportunities.

7. *Develop right- and left-brain hybrids.* A hybrid system focused on leadership through emotional intelligence and scientific and technical excellence was instrumental in building up collaboration, productivity, teamwork, and quality surgical teams while lowering conflict, grievances, and communication problems.

8. *Educate the patient/customer.* Educating patients about the full range of possibilities and expectations dealt with the small incidence of patient dissatisfaction with surgical decision-making.

9. *Close abundance gaps through cross fertilization and training.* Surgeons, cardiologists, nurses, anesthesiologists, technicians, and staff were all trained in the intricacies of minimal-incision mitral valve procedures as a prerequisite to serving as faculty in the program. Dr. Lorimer and Dr. Zaroff combined forces to close critical abundance gaps by turning open-heart surgeries into tutorials and training classes for fellow surgeons and staff directly involved in serving on surgical teams. Another abundance gap was revealed by a small percentage of dissatisfied patients and led to the creation of pre- and postoperative psychological counseling services to serve ethical, religious, emotional, and relationship concerns pertaining to surgeries and outcomes.

10. *Give awards for "positive deviance."* Under the leadership of Dr. Lorimer and Dr. Zaroff the hospital established "Positive Deviance Awards" for staff-generated innovations designed to further advance the minimal-incision mitral valve procedure; to date there have been eleven applications and three awards presented for significant innovations and research and development; awards are sanctioned by upper echelon leadership, and prizes include money and professional recognition.

11. *Establish leadership mentoring and development programs.* Under the leadership of Dr. Lorimer and Dr. Zaroff, Eisenhower Heart Institute initiated "Outreach for Excellence Programs." Cardiologists from around the world train under the two surgeons as "shadows" during open-heart procedures; this serves the quest for abundance and superior performance by diffusing the mitral valve procedures to surgeons and other centers of excellence.

12. *Prioritize social and emotional intelligence in performance reviews.* Under the leadership of Dr. Zaroff and the director of HR, an abundance gap in supportive communication, emotional intelligence, and social intelligence was narrowed by instituting an alternative to the traditional annual performance appraisal. This once-a-year evaluation was initially replaced by quarterly reviews and then by a monthly "management performance interview" placing highest priority on relationship and people skills.

13. *Provide collaborative in-house training and development.* Training and development in emotional intelligence, social intelligence, emotional competence, negotiation, and conflict resolution following the principles developed by the Harvard Negotiation Project.

14. *Hire toxin detectors and toxin handlers.* The resilient organization must be able to achieve early detection of unhealthy, toxic, and dysfunctional behaviors. Instead of having to make ninth-inning calls to external consultants and coaches, toxin detectors can preserve excellence by making such calls early in the game. At Eisenhower, in an effort to close a serious abundance gap, leadership in cardiology, HR, training and development, and EAP banded together to formally train what Peter Frost (2003) called "toxin detectors" and "toxin healers."

15. *Adopt a culture of abundance.* As part of Dr. Avi Zaroff's initial briefings in preparation for assuming leadership of cardiology's roundtable meetings, the doctor was provided with T&D simulations of negative deviance, now conceived as abundance gaps. The trainers and Dr. Zaroff concentrated on the strengths of all members, building on them and moving toward collaborative dialogue.

16. *Adopt a language of abundance.* Evaluate official documents and informal daily communication and reformulate them using positive language rather than a language of negatives and deficits.

17. *Formulate the top ten "abundance gaps."* Organizational deficits were reformulated as abundance gaps via a new series of training and development programs provided by in-house specialists. At Eisenhower, T&D specialists were briefed on the top ten abundance gaps experienced by surgical teams under the leadership of Dr. Lorimer; the "step in your colleague's shoes" simulations and role playing have reduced aggression, impatience, suspicion, and built patience, trust, and appreciation between colleagues.

18. *Build teams through cross-fertilization.* Establish mandatory once-a-week cross-fertilization meetings for directors and leaders of departments and

divisions. Leaders should become increasingly and eventually thoroughly familiar with each other's expertise. Each meeting should give each attendee two minutes to address his or her best or most challenging business and leadership experiences over the past month. Attendees brainstorm how to transform extreme deficit behavior or the most toxic business experience into an opportunity.

19. *Adopt an incremental small-wins strategy.* Use project management teams to point out small wins and promote an abundance consciousness that does not succumb to disappointments from the past or prior deficits in the organization.

20. *Develop a culture of collaborative communication.* Under the leadership of the training and development and HR divisions, mini training sessions and speechmaking opportunities must attempt to promote excellence in communication; this should entail early, preemptive information sharing.

21. *Act, don't just talk.* In closing abundance gaps, meetings and discussions do not take the place of action.

22. *Establish metrics and performance targets.* The establishment of metrics for measurement of productivity, quality, and defects can offset burnout, red flag "issues of concern," and close out any abundance gaps surrounding meaning and purposefulness. Set performance targets for zero defects.

23. *Use true narratives to build a collaborative culture.* Closing abundance gaps frequently entails making the invisible visible and telling the "rest of the story" via case histories and narratives.

FINAL WORDS

Troubled organizations often have invested heavily in their areas of technical expertise but have overlooked emotional and social intelligence. For those, I often recommend a shift from conducting annual performance appraisals to holding quarterly or even monthly "management performance interviews." Assuming that leadership and the organizational culture are not overly inhospitable to the human dimension, I suggest that a significant increase in the dialogue between leaders, managers, professionals, and staff is preferable to a once-a-year assessment. Going one step further, Eisenhower Heart Institute initiated a "toxin detector" and "toxin handler" program with two HR people cast in those roles. Constant attendance to the psychological and social dramas in the workplace is preferable to a production-only mentality or an extreme "no emotions allowed" mandate.

But even under the best of circumstances toxicity will surface. As demonstrated throughout this book, there is ample reason to believe that interpersonal contamination is more likely to originate in the organizational system than in the "rotten apple in the barrel" leader. Even dictatorial and ruthless managers often are being directed or protected by a CEO, president, or executive board fueling the tyrant's behavior. Complex webs of toxic relationships develop in organizations in part owing to impoverished systems low in emotional intelligence and in part owing to variables such as disparities, hurtful and demeaning policies, negligent leaders who attempt to sweep conflict under the rug, and a myriad of dysfunctional people issues.

As a leadership coach and consultant I rarely offer quick assessments or solutions; nor do I rely overly on so-called evidence-based objective assessment tools such as questionnaires and standardized audits. I depend primarily on in-person observation over extended periods of time, multiple structured interviews with leaders and employees, examination of multiple documents including e-mails, contracts, newsletters, and work products, and the analysis of available quality metrics.

In several of the cases presented in this book the companies called in external experts only after the leadership had reluctantly acknowledged the seriousness of the organizational toxicity. Late calls typically involve higher levels of toxicity. In the Jarling-Weber case it was actually too late to save a highly dictatorial set of leaders and an organization that was already dying. Scolding and scathing in their approach to the consultants, the firm's leaders attempted to dictate their agenda to the outside expert. This is usually a bad idea. Surely a consultant or coach who is worth calling in the first place should be extended the opportunity to metaphorically place the stethoscope on the corporate patient and derive a differential diagnosis. This option was never extended to the consultant hired by Jarling-Weber, and within two years the company was bankrupt. The moral of the story is that a genuine dialogue based on honesty, trust, and collaboration is essential between coach and client. There is no substitute. Ironically, however, the CEO of Jarling-Weber was more than salvageable. The consultant was able to serve Mr. Lunger in the capacity of a leadership coach, in part influencing his decision to resign from Jarling-Weber and pursue other opportunities.

The EuroText and Eisenhower consultations offer immediate takeaways for coaches and clients. Innovation and resourcefulness are extremely important when attempting to find an antidote to trauma, organizational pain, and toxicity. At first, both the EuroText and Eisenhower leaders were entrenched, defensive, and protective of their self-destructive behavior and policies. They resisted any tampering with an established pattern of negative organizational behavior. Only through novel and creative approaches did the consultant break through their resistance. With EuroText that meant brainstorming to reach a hybrid solution. At Eisenhower it took recasting a perceived problem and breaking the organizational mold.

Overall, I urge organizations to seriously heed the human dimension. Pay constant and ample attention to human communication, interpersonal and team relations, the building of a culture of collaboration rather than silos of divisiveness, and the development of designated toxin detectors and handlers. Unattended, an everyday altercation can fester and turn a division against itself. Years of avoidance escalate the poisons. Vendettas and edicts will not eradicate angry, spiritless, unmotivated, agitated, and sabotage-minded professionals. If toxic thoughts, emotions, and behaviors cannot be adequately addressed from within your walls, then an external management consultant or leadership coach may be able to provide a fresh assessment and break the stalemate. Even where deep division and conflict bordering on trauma has set in, keep in mind that there is always a prospect for post-traumatic growth. Even the darkest moments and most hopeless conversations can provide opportunities for positive transformation. For leaders and organizations stuck in destructive policies and patterns of behavior, the guided transition from deficit to abundance can offer a transformational alternative. I hope that the stories of the leaders and companies presented in this book, and the recommendations for reducing organizational toxicity, will contribute to the widespread achievement of personal and organizational health.

Reference Matter

Glossary

abundance leadership: A type of leadership characterized by its commitment to positive behavior and the pursuit of the highest individual and organizational outcomes; rather than being consumed by difficulties, obstacles, problems, and a deficit approach to change, abundance leadership is committed to developing people's strengths, finding possibilities, building potential, and improving processes.

Americans with Disabilities Act (ADA): The ADA protects individuals from discrimination in the workplace on the basis of a qualifying disability. Impairments covered by the ADA, Section 504, include mental and psychological disorders, mental retardation, organic brain syndrome, and specific learning disabilities.

assessment: The management consultant conducts a case history, collects data, and may engage in direct observation or field studies in order to develop an assessment of an organization's strengths, weaknesses, opportunities, and threats; the assessment is typically viewed as the first step in a consultation.

attention deficit disorder (ADD): An official disorder included in the *Diagnostic and Statistical Manual of Mental Illnesses* (DSM IV-TR) identifying a longstanding dysfunctional approach to perception epitomized by: erratic responses to stimuli; an inability to adequately focus on individual objects or subjects; a long-term pattern of appearing "spaced out" and not fully engaged in the matters unfolding in the room; an appearance of being physically present but mentally absent or vacant despite surface engagement; and an ongoing difficulty paying ample attention to information and persons present.

attention deficit/hyperactivity disorder (ADHD): A psychological disorder cited in the DSM IV-TR referring to long-term difficulties focusing attention fully on vital persons, actions, and activities and marked by a "jumping around" in perception; in addition to the inability to focus on one person or situation at a time, the ADHD client also experiences hyperactivity or exaggerated stimulation and appears to be in constant motion as if driven by a large and constantly running motor.

brief rapid-cycle therapy: A fast-lane, short-term, drive-by approach to diagnosing and treating individual psychological problems and pathologies displayed in the workplace.

client privilege: Confidentiality extended and guaranteed by law to an individual organizational member who is a client or patient of a professional counselor or psychologist; in the case of a diagnosis of a mental or emotional disorder, client privilege remains in place unless the counselor determines that the client is a danger to self (DTS) or a danger to others (DTO) in the organization; also referred to as "privileged communication."

collaborative leadership: A team-oriented and horizontal approach to leadership characterized by the empowerment of a number of selected individuals in the decision-making, power, and influence process.

confidentiality: See "client privilege."

corporate mask: A superficial public identity designed for impression management; a corporate veneer for mass consumption that conceals behaviors and true motives.

danger to others (DTO): Central to a psychological evaluation of an employee or leader is the determination whether the individual is presently or potentially a danger to others; if the psychologist or consultant determines that a leader is a DTO, then this diagnosis results in a waiving of privileged communication and confidentiality rights; a report of the diagnosis is made to the appropriate member(s) of the organization.

danger to self (DTS): Central to a psychological evaluation of an employee or leader is the determination whether the individual is presently or potentially a danger to self; if the psychologist or consultant determines that a leader is a DTS, then this diagnosis results in a waiving of privileged communication and confidentiality rights; a report of the diagnosis is made to the appropriate member(s) of the organization;

demagoguery: An extreme form of hierarchical, centralized leadership marked by edicts, ultimatums, raw and unadulterated power over a workforce, and an aversion to discussion, debate, or substantive input in decision-making.

destructive leadership: Leadership behavior to the detriment of the organization with the potential for producing toxicity.

detox/detoxification: Specific assessments, diagnoses, and intervention strategies to reduce, control, and/or eliminate destructive and toxic behaviors of individual leaders and entire organizations.

diagnosis: A clinical assessment of an individual leader or organizational member by a trained and certified counselor, psychologist, or other mental health professional utilizing recognized and sanctioned diagnostic criteria (e.g., as listed in the DSM IV-TR).

differential diagnosis: Influenced by systems analysis of organizations and multifaceted diagnoses of physicians, the differential diagnosis investigates origins and instigators of reported company problems, conflicts, and crises; evaluations assume a potential for complex multiple causality involving leadership behavior, departments, policies, and systemwide interaction as strategic to a comprehensive assessment of organizational dysfunction, and/or toxicity.

DSM IV-TR (*Diagnostic and Statistical Manual of Mental Illnesses*): A clinical manual used in the diagnosis of mental and emotional disturbances; recognized as a source of objective criteria and the world standard for diagnoses of mental illness.

dysfunctional organizational behavior: Impaired and destructive behavior, leadership and/or policies with negative impact on productivity, workplace relationships, and teams; below functional behavior working contrary to positive organizational outcomes.

emotional contagion: The transmission from person to person, almost like a disease, of positive and negative emotions.

emotional intelligence: The ability to identify and constructively manage one's own emotions and those of others in a group or organization; also an interdisciplinary area of research addressed to the right-brain, intuitive, affective, aesthetic and artistic, and research and development side of leadership and organizational behavior.

emotional toxicity: Toxicity rooted in destructive emotions in the workplace, typically witnessed in workplace conflicts or emanating from dysfunctional leadership.

Everest goals: high and lofty leadership and organizational goals rooted in positive psychology and referring metaphorically to the heights of Mt. Everest.

Harvard Negotiation Project: A world-class approach to the negotiation process developed at Harvard University by Harvard faculty and rooted in a book by

Fisher, Ury, and Patton entitled *Getting to Yes: Negotiating Agreement Without Giving In.*

hypodermic needle model of consulting: A phrase used in management consulting circles to refer to the corporate client and/or consultant who subscribes to an extreme hierarchical, expert-knows-best approach to consultation; the hypodermic needle model metaphorically refers to the consultant-as-doctor who injects the client-as-patient with the information, knowledge, and interventions necessary to transform organizational sickness to health.

intentionally toxic behavior: Central to the identification of toxic behavior is the strategic determination whether destructive leader and/or organizational behaviors are intentional or unintentional; intentionally toxic behavior is strategically intended to bully, harm, rape, injure, or otherwise be purposefully destructive toward intended targets.

intermittent explosive disorder (IED): A long-term, repetitive anger management problem characterized by verbal and nonverbal public outbursts directed toward colleagues and/or subordinates; the IED individual is temporarily loud and emotionally enraged, and may be perceived as a physical threat; IED individuals are typically remorseful about their explosiveness; IED is the most common form of psychopathology and toxic behavior among corporate and organizational leaders.

internal coach: An official coach provided by an organization's employee assistance program (EAP), or a manager or colleague who unofficially assumes a coaching role in the workplace.

intervention: Specific actions or interventions based on assessment, observation, testing, and field studies by a management consultant or leadership coach; interventions represent strategic actions for positive leadership and organizational change.

intoxication: A mental and emotional state characterized by poor reasoning, irrationality, and destructive behavior; when the toxic leader's destructive behavior spreads throughout an organization his followers may become intoxicated.

leader detox training: Specific strategies and interventions intended to reduce destructive behavior and leader toxicity to normative or positive levels.

leadership-by-edict: See "demagoguery."

leadership coach: An expert who typically provides one-on-one instruction, dialogue, and counsel to develop and enhance the positive leadership skills of the client and decrease and control the negative and destructive behaviors.

left-brain leadership: A predominantly logical, rational, analytical, and highly reasoned approach to and dimension of leadership.

management by walking around (MBWA): A physically engaging approach to managing characterized by a high degree of interpersonal involvement with employees; a face-to-face physical relationship between management and workers is central to MBWA.

management consultant: A trained expert who serves leadership and organizational clients through assessment, diagnosis, companywide change, and interventions.

medical model of consulting: Characterized by the positioning of the consultant as a "doctor" and the organization as a "patient" in an exchange highlighted by the doctor's expertise and the patient's sickness; leaders and the company as a whole position themselves as inactive and passive and wait for the expert to perform an intervention that will lead to the healing of the illness and a return to organizational health.

micromanagement by walking around: Obsessive, minutiae-oriented management characterized by a failure to trust or empower employees to perform a myriad of minor tasks.

narcissism: An overindulgence in the self; a narcissistic leader is more concerned about her own self-worth, appearance, and/or ability to be admired and respected than about the well-being and success of her organization or colleagues.

narcissistic personality disorder: A long-term repetitive pattern of behavior characterized by redundant self-indulgence in one's appearance or other dimension of the self, marked by the spending of exorbitant amounts of time to feed the all-consuming narcissistic obsession; feeding and sustaining one's own needs and desires takes priority over all other dimensions of work and social life.

organizational misbehavior (OMB): A research focus and orientation in the professional academic and applied management and leadership literature focusing on behaviors that are detrimental to an organization's task and relationship goals; the systematic study of misbehavior in organizations.

organizational pathology: A term advanced by Jurgen Ruesch and Gregory Bateson referring to the diffusion of mental and emotional disturbances throughout an organization; sometimes rooted in the individual pathology of a leader, the excesses and mental disturbance of a single leader may morph into departmental, divisional, and organizational pathologies (e.g., ADHD; obsessive-compulsive disorder; narcissistic personality disorder; antisocial personality disorder).

organizational therapy: A variety of management consulting focused on psychological and emotional disturbances within the organization with the purpose of providing accurate diagnoses, interventions, and therapy.

personality disorders: A category of deeply rooted psychological disturbances or mental illnesses cited in the DSM IV-TR and including but not limited to: narcissistic personality disorder; obsessive compulsive personality disorder; and antisocial personality disorder.

post-traumatic stress disorder (PTSD): Once popularly referred to as "shell shock," PTSD refers to mental and emotional disturbances rooted in and traceable to traumatic incidents such as murder, war, disfigurement, and violent death experiences.

privileged communication: See "client privilege."

psychobabble: Incoherent, misleading, mistaken, or superficial pseudo-psychological assessment and talk about behavior in the workplace; an attempt to psychologically interpret motives and behaviors without adequate training, insight, or merit.

psychopathological leadership: Leadership characterized by extremely destructive behavior and attributable to mental and emotional disorders cited in the DSM IV-TR.

right-brain leadership: Leadership characterized by emotional intelligence, intuition, and artistic and innovative dimensions.

rotten apples: Individual employees, colleagues, or leaders singled out as the direct cause of destructive, dysfunctional, and toxic organizational behavior.

shell shock: See "post-traumatic stress disorder."

Six Sigma: An outgrowth of the quality movement and total quality control (TQC) and total quality management (TQM), Six Sigma is a controlled process that strategizes toward and is committed to zero defects (ZDs); the technical quality control goal is to achieve no defects within six standard deviations of the target level of performance—which translates into 3.4 defects per million units—or in practical terms, zero defects.

theory X: A traditional, centralized, and authoritarian approach to organizational leadership characterized by a vertical and hierarchical structuring of power and influence.

theory Y: A decentralized, horizontal, and empowerment approach to organizational leadership characterized by many voices and inputs in decision-making and influence.

360-degree feedback: Also called multi-rater assessment, multi-source assessment, and multi-source feedback, 360-degree feedback is collected systemically—from peers and colleagues, superiors, subordinates, and internal and external customers. The primary objective of 360 is to assess training and development needs and to provide multi-faceted, multi-dimensional, companywide data central to a competence-based appraisal for succession planning.

total quality management (TQM): A comprehensive and companywide approach to continuous improvement of all products and services; TQM is everybody's business as all organizational members throughout the hierarchy and across specializations are linked together in a common pursuit of quality and getting it right the first time; policies, allocation of resources, production, quality control measures, performance appraisals, and ongoing monitoring of results are dimensions of the overall TQM engine that drives excellence.

toxic downsizing: A downsizing that feeds into depression, anger, insecurities, and fears of workers; when released workers feel demeaned, trivialized, and disrespected in the process of a downsizing, predictable levels of pain figure in a toxic pattern that spreads among employees and invites retaliation against perceived perpetrators.

toxic leadership: Destructive, disturbing, and dysfunctional acts of supervision that spread among members of the workforce.

toxin detector: According to Frost (2003), an individual who arises within an organization who is perceived as being an extremely good listener, empathic, emotionally intelligent, and trustworthy to the extent that he or she is sought out by members of the workforce for advice and confidential communication; the toxin detector is able to assist colleagues with their concerns over destructive and dysfunctional thoughts, emotions, and relationships and help them assess their concerns and troubles.

toxin healer: A toxin detector may also function as a toxin healer (Frost 2003), offering colleagues a therapeutic ear and guidance out of troubling and potentially destructive behavior; the healer functions unofficially as a lay psychologist or psychiatrist and is typically endowed with high levels of emotional intelligence, listening skills, empathy, and compassion, but may lack formal training.

transformational leader: A leader who inspires, motivates, and uplifts an organization's members so that they can excel and approach loftier heights in process and production; a transformational leader is able to positively change or move the organization and its membership to a higher ground by inspiring character-building and the development of interpersonal and presentational skills.

unintentionally toxic behavior: Typically misunderstood or trivialized, unintentionally toxic behavior is individual behavior that has had a detrimental effect on customers, superiors, or colleagues; unintentionally toxic behavior may have its origins in mental and emotional disturbances such as adult attention deficit/hyperactivity disorder (ADHD); the individual may act in an unintentionally irritating or destructive manner in the workplace, without full awareness of same; this can be addressed via professional diagnosis and intervention.

References

Ackroyd, S., and P. Thompson. 1999. *Organizational Misbehavior*. London: Sage.

American Psychiatric Association. 2000. *Diagnostic and Statistical Manual of Mental Disorders—DSM IV-TR*. 4th rev. ed. Arlington, Va.: American Psychiatric Association.

Analoui, F. 1995. "Workplace Sabotage: Its Styles, Motives and Management." *Journal of Management Development* 14 (7): 48–65.

Argyris, C. 2004. *Reasons and Rationalizations: The Limits to Organizational Knowledge*. New York: Oxford University Press.

Babiak, P., and R. Hare. 2006. *Snakes in Suits: When Psychopaths Go to Work*. New York: Regan Books/Harper Collins.

Bakan, J. 2004. *The Corporation*. New York: Free Press.

Baron, R. 1990. "Countering the Effects of Destructive Criticism." *Journal of Applied Psychology* 75 (33): 235–245.

Barrick, M. R., and M. K. Mount. 1991. "The Big Five Personality Dimensions and Job Performance." *Personnel Psychology* 44: 1–26.

Basch, J., and C. Fisher. 2000. "Affective Events-Emotions Matrix: A Classification of Job-Related Events and Emotions Experienced in the Workplace." In N. Ashkanasy, W. Zerbe, and C. Hartel, eds., *Emotions in the Workplace: Research, Theory and Practice*, pp. 36–48. Westport, Conn.: Quorum Books.

Bateson, G. 1969. "Pathologies of Epistemology." Paper presented at the Second Conference on Mental Health in Asia and the Pacific, East-West Center, Honolulu.

————. 1972. *Steps to an Ecology of Mind*. New York: Ballantine.

Block, J., and A. Kremen. 1996. "IQ and Ego-Resiliency: Conceptual and Empirical Connections and Separateness." *Journal of Personality and Social Psychology* 70: 349–361.

Block, P., and A. Markowitz. 2000. *The Flawless Consulting Fieldbook and Companion*. New York: John Wiley.

Bradford, D. L., and W. Burke. 2005a. *The Crisis in Organizational Development*. San Francisco, Calif.: Jossey-Bass.

———. 2005b. *Reinventing Organization Development: New Approaches to Change in Organizations*. San Francisco: Pfeiffer.

Bright, D., K. Cameron, and A. Caza. 2006. "The Amplifying and Buffering Effects of Virtuousness in Downsized Organizations." *Journal of Business Ethics* 64: 249–269.

Brown, S. 2000. "The Stresses of Clinical Medicine." In D. Haslam, ed., *Not Another Guide to Stress in General Practice!* Oxford: Radcliffe Medical Press.

Buber, M. 1965. "Elements of the Interhuman." In M. Friedman, ed., *The Knowledge of Man*. New York: Harper and Row.

———. 1970. *I and Thou*. New York: Charles Scribner's Sons.

Burke, W. 2002. *Organization Change: Theory and Practice*. Thousand Oaks, Calif.: Sage.

Buss, D. 1999. *Evolutionary Psychology: The New Science of the Mind*. Needham Heights, Mass.: Allyn and Bacon.

Cameron, K. 1994. "Strategies for Successful Organizational Downsizing." *Human Resource Management* 33 (2): 189–211.

Cameron, K., and M. Lavine. 2006. *Making the Impossible Possible: Leading Extraordinary Performance—The Rocky Flats Story*. San Francisco: Berrett-Koehler.

Cameron, K., and R. Quinn. 2006. *Diagnosing and Changing Organizational Culture: Based on the Competing Values Framework*. San Francisco: Jossey-Bass.

Cameron, K., J. Dutton, and R. Quinn. 2003. *Positive Organizational Scholarship*. San Francisco: Berrett-Koehler.

Clair, J., and R. Dufresne. 2007. "Changing Poison into Medicine: How Companies Can Experience Positive Transformation from a Crisis." *Organizational Dynamics* 36 (1): 63–77.

Clark, T., and R. Fincham. 2002. *Critical Consulting: New Perspectives on the Management Advice Industry*. Oxford: Blackwell Business Press.

Clifton, D., and J. Harter. 2003. "Investing in Strengths." In K. Cameron, J. Sutton, R. Quinn, eds., *Positive Organizational Scholarship: Foundation of a New Discipline*, pp. 111–121. San Francisco: Berrett-Koehler.

Cloninger, C. R. 1987. "A Systematic Method for Clinical Description and Classification of Personality Variants: A Proposal." *Archives of General Psychiatry* 44: 573–588.

Compernolle, T. 2007. "Developmental Coaching from a Systems Point of View." In M. Kets De Vries, K. Korotov, and E. Florent-Treacy, eds., *Coach and Couch: The Psychology of Making Better Leaders*. Houndmills, Basingstoke, Hampshire, U.K.: Palgrave Macmillan.

Conger, J., and R. Kanungo, R. 1987. "Toward a Behavioral Theory of Charismatic Leadership in Organizational Settings." *Academy of Management Review* 12: 637–647.

Coombs, R., and F. Fawzy. 1986. "The Impaired-Physician Syndrome: A Developmental Perspective." In C. Scott and J. Hawk, eds., *Heal Thyself*. New York: Brunner/Mazel.

Cooperrider, D., P. Sorensen, D. Whitney, and T. Yaeger. 2000. *Appreciative Inquiry: Rethinking Human Organization: Toward a Positive Theory of Change.* Champaign, Ill.: Stipes.

Crino, M., and T. Leap. 1989. "What HR Managers Must Know about Employee Sabotage." *Personnel* 66 (5): 31–38.

Dunnette, M., and L. Hough, eds. 1992. *Handbook of Industrial and Organizational Psychology.* Palo Alto, Calif.: Consulting Psychology Press.

Ekman, P., and R. Davidson, eds. 1994. *The Nature of Emotion: Fundamental Questions.* New York: Oxford University Press.

Engellau, E. 2007. "The Dos and Don'ts of Coaching: Key Lessons I Learned as an Executive Coach." In M. Kets de Vries, K. Korotov, and E. Florent-Treacy, eds., *Coach and Couch*, pp. 240–254. Houndmills, Basingstoke, Hampshire, U.K.: Palgrave Macmillan.

Farson, R. 1997. *Management of the Absurd: Paradoxes in Leadership.* New York: Touchstone.

Fineman, S. 1996. "Emotion and Organizing." In S. Clegg, C. Hardy, and W. Nord, eds., *Handbook of Organization Studies*, pp. 543–564. London: Sage.

Fisher, R., W. Ury, and B. Patton. 1991. *Getting to Yes: Negotiating Agreement Without Giving In.* New York: Penguin.

Fitzgerald, T., H. Tennen, G. Affleck, and G. Pransky. 1993. "The Relative Importance of Dispositional Optimism and Control Appraisals in Quality of Life after Coronary Artery Bypass Surgery." *Journal of Behavioral Medicine* 16: 25–43.

Fox, S., and P. Spector. 2005. *Counterproductive Work Behavior: Investigations of Actors and Targets.* Washington, D.C.: American Psychological Association.

Frankl, V. 1960. "Paradoxical Intention." *American Journal of Psychotherapy* 14: 520–535.

Frederickson, B. 2003. "The Value of Positive Emotions." *American Scientist* 91 (4): 330–335.

Frost, P. 2003. *Toxic Emotions in the Workplace: How Compassionate Managers Handle Pain and Conflict.* Boston: Harvard Business School Press.

Frost, P., and S. Robinson. 1999. "The Toxic Handler: Organizational Hero—and Casualty." *Harvard Business Review* (July–August): 97–106.

Fuqua, D., and J. Newman. 2002. "The Role of Systems Theory in Consulting Psychology." In R. Lowman, ed., *Handbook of Organizational Consulting Psychology.* San Francisco: Jossey-Bass.

Gallessich, J. 1982. *The Profession and Practice of Consultation.* San Francisco: Jossey-Bass.

Gladwell, M. 2005. *Blink: The Power of Thinking Without Thinking.* New York: Little, Brown.

Goldman, A. 1994. *Doing Business with the Japanese: A Guide to Successful Communication, Management and Diplomacy.* Albany: State University of New York Press.

———. 2005. "Leadership Pathology as a Nexus of Dysfunctional Organizations." Paper presented at the Academy of Management Conference, Honolulu.

———. 2006a. "Personality Disorders in Leaders: Implications of the DSM IV-TR in Assessing Dysfunctional Organizations." *Journal of Managerial Psychology* 21 (5): 392–414.

———. 2006b. "High Toxicity Leadership: Borderline Personality Disorder and the Dysfunctional Organization." *Journal of Managerial Psychology* 21 (8): 733–746.

———. 2007. "Leadership Negligence and Malpractice: Emotional Unintelligence at SkyWaves Aerospace International." Paper presented at the Academy of Management Conference, Philadelphia.

———. 2008a. "Leadership Negligence and Malpractice: Emotional Toxicity at Skywaves Aerospace International." In W. Zerbe, C. Hartel, and N. Ashkanasy, eds., *Research on Emotion in Organizations*, Volume 4: *Emotions, Ethics and Decision-Making*, pp. 207–224. Bingley, U.K.: Emerald.

———. 2008b. "Company on the Couch: Unveiling Toxic Behavior in Dysfunctional Organizations." *Journal of Management Inquiry* 17 (3): 226–238.

Goldsmith, M., L. Lyons, and A. Freas, eds. 2000. *Coaching for Leadership*. San Francisco: Jossey-Bass.

Goleman, D., 1995. *Emotional Intelligence*. New York: Bantam.

———. 2000. *Working with Emotional Intelligence*. New York: Bantam.

———. 2006. *Social Intelligence: The New Science of Human Relationships*. New York: Bantam Books.

Goleman, D., R. Boyatzis, and A. McKee. 2002. *Primal Leadership: Learning to Lead with Emotional Intelligence*. Boston: Harvard Business School Press.

Gunderson, L. 2001. "Physician Burnout." *Annals of Internal Medicine* 135: 145–148.

Haley, J. 1963. *Strategies of Psychotherapy*. New York: Grune and Stratton.

Henriques, J., and R. Davidson. 1997. "Brain Electrical Asymmetries During Cognitive Task Performance in Depressed and Nondepressed Subjects." *Biological Psychiatry* 42: 1039–1050.

Hollinger, R., and J. Clark, 1982. "Employee Deviance: A Response to the Perceived Quality of the Work Experience." *Work and Occupations* 9: 97–114.

James, E., and L. Wooten. 2005. "Leadership as (Un)Usual: How to Display Competence in Times of Crisis." *Organizational Dynamics* 34 (2): 141–152.

Kellerman, B. 2004. *Bad Leadership: What It Is, How It Happens, Why It Matters*. Boston: Harvard Business School Press.

Kets de Vries, M. 1984. *The Irrational Executive: Psychoanalytic Explorations in Management*. Madison, Conn.: International Universities Press.

———. 1995. *Life and Death in the Executive Fast Lane*. San Francisco: Jossey-Bass.

———. 2006. *The Leader on the Couch: A Clinical Approach to Changing People and Organizations*. San Francisco: Jossey-Bass.

Kets de Vries, M., and Associates. 1991. *Organizations on the Couch: Clinical Perspectives on Organizational Behavior and Change.* San Francisco: Jossey-Bass.

Kets de Vries, M., and D. Miller. 1984. *The Neurotic Organization: Diagnosing and Changing Counterproductive Styles of Management.* San Francisco: Jossey-Bass.

Kilburg, R. 2000. *Executive Coaching: Developing Managerial Wisdom in a World of Chaos.* Washington, D.C.: American Psychological Society.

Kipping, M., and L. Engwall. 2002. *Management Consulting: Emergence and Dynamics of a Knowledge Industry.* Oxford: Oxford University Press.

Kolb, D., and J. Williams. 2003. *Everyday Negotiations: Navigating the Hidden Agendas in Bargaining.* San Francisco: Jossey-Bass.

Koortzen, P., and F. Cilliers. 2002. "The Psychoanalytic Approach to Team Development." In R. Lowman, ed., *Handbook of Organizational Consulting Psychology.* San Francisco: Jossey-Bass.

Lachman, V. 1983. *Stress Management: A Manual for Nurses.* New York: Grune and Stratton.

Lawler, E. 2000. *Rewarding Excellence: Pay Strategies for the New Economy.* San Francisco: Jossey-Bass.

Lazarus, R. 1991. *Emotion and Adaptation.* New York: Oxford University Press.

Levinson, H. 1972. *Organizational Diagnosis.* Cambridge, Mass.: Harvard University Press.

———. 1976. *Psychological Man.* Boston: Levinson Institute.

———. 1981. *Executive.* Cambridge, Mass.: Harvard University Press.

———. 1987. "Psychoanalytic Theory in Organizational Behavior." In J. W. Lorsch, ed., *Handbook of Organizational Behavior.* Englewood Cliffs, N.J.: Prentice Hall.

———. 2002. *Organizational Assessment: A Step-by-Step Guide to Effective Consulting.* Washington, D.C.: American Psychological Association.

Lipman-Blumen, J. 2005. *The Allure of Toxic Leaders.* New York: Oxford University Press.

Lowman, R., ed. 2002. *Handbook of Organizational and Consulting Psychology.* San Francisco: Jossey-Bass.

Lubit, R. 2004. *Coping with Toxic Managers, Subordinates . . . and Other Difficult People.* Englewood Cliffs, N.J.: Financial Times / Prentice Hall.

Luthans, F., and B. Avolio. 2003. "Authentic Leadership: A Positive Development Approach." In K. Cameron, J. Dutton, and R. Quinn, eds., *Positive Organizational Scholarship,* pp. 241–258. San Francisco: Berrett-Koehler.

Luthans, F., B. Avolio, F. Walumbwa, and W. Li. 2005. "The Psychological Capital of Chinese Workers: Exploring the Relationship of Performance." *Management and Organization Review* 1: 249–271.

Luthans, F., C. Youssef, and B. Avolio. 2007a. *Psychological Capital: Developing the Human Competitive Edge.* New York: Oxford University Press.

————. 2007b. "Psychological Capital: Investing and Developing Positive Organizational Behavior." In D. Nelson and C. Cooper, eds., *Positive Organizational Behavior*. London: Sage.

Maccoby, M. 2007. *Narcissistic Leaders: Who Succeeds and Who Fails*. Boston: Harvard Business School Press.

Masten, A. 2001. "Ordinary Magic: Resilience Processes in Development." *American Psychologist* 56: 227–239.

Masten, A., and M. Reed. 2002. "Resilience in Development." In C. Snyder and J. Lopez, eds., *Handbook of Positive Psychology*, pp. 74–88. London: Oxford University Press.

Mayer, R., J. Davis, and D. Schoorman. 1995. "An Integrative Model of Organizational Trust." *Academy of Management Review* 20: 709–734.

McCraty, R., and M. Atkinson. 1995. "The Physiological and Psychological Effects of Compassion and Anger." *Journal of Advancement in Medicine* 8 (2): 87–105.

McDermott, D., and C. Snyder. 1999. *Making Hope Happen*. Oakland, Calif.: New Harbinger.

McGregor, D. 1985. *The Human Side of Enterprise*. New York: McGraw-Hill.

Mee, C. 2002. "Battling Burnout." *Nursing* 32 (8): 8.

Merleau-Ponty, M. 2004. *Phenomenology of Perception*. New York: Routledge.

Michael, S. 2000. "Hope Conquers Fear: Overcoming Anxiety and Panic Attacks." In C. Snyder, ed., *Handbook of Hope: Theory, Measures, and Applications*. San Diego, Calif.: Academic Press, 355–378.

Miller, D. 1981. "Towards a New Contingency Approach: The Search for Organizational Gestalts." *Journal of Management Studies* 18 (1): 1–26.

Miller, D., and C. Droge. 1986. "Psychological and Traditional Determinants of Structure." *Administrative Science Quarterly* 31: 539–560.

Miller, D., and J. M. Toulouse. 1986. "Strategy, Structure, CEO Personality, and Performance in Small Firms." *American Journal of Small Business* 11: 47–62.

Miller, D., M. Kets de Vries, and J. Toulouse. 1982. "Top Executive Locus of Control and Its Relationship to Strategy Making, Structure and Environment." *Academy of Management Journal* 25: 237–253.

Minuchin, S. 1974. *Families and Family Therapy*. Cambridge, Mass.: Harvard University Press.

Nelson, D., and C. Cooper. 2007. *Positive Organizational Behavior*. London: Sage.

Neuman, J. 2001. "Injustice, Stress and Bullying Can Be Expensive!" Presentation at Workplace Bullying 2000 Conference, Oakland, Calif.

Obholzer, A. 1994. "Authority, Power and Leadership." In A. Obholzer and V. Roberts, eds., *The Unconscious at Work*. London: Routledge.

Ozcelik, H., and S. Maitlis. 2001. "Toxic Decision Making: The Mismanagement of Emotional Issues in Organizations." Paper presented at the Academy of Management Annual Meeting, Washington, D.C.

Peterson, S., F. Walumbwa, K. Byron, and J. Myrowitz. 2008 "CEO Positive Psychological Traits, Transformational Leadership, and Firm Performance in High-Technology Start-up and Established Firms." *Journal of Management* 20 (4): 1–21.

Pfeffer, J., and R. Sutton. 2006. *Hard Facts, Dangerous Half-Truths, and Total Nonsense: Profiting from Evidence-Based Management.* Boston: Harvard Business School Press.

Pfifferling, J. 1986. "Cultural Antecedents Promoting Professional Impairment." In C. Scott and J. Hawk, eds., *Heal Thyself: The Health of Health Care Professionals.* New York: Brunner Mazel.

Potter-Efron, R. 1998. *Working Anger: Preventing and Resolving Conflict on the Job.* Oakland, Calif.: New Harbinger.

Reinhold, B. 1997. *Toxic Work.* New York: Plume.

Rice, V., ed. 2000. *Handbook of Stress, Coping and Health: Implications for Nursing Research, Theory and Practice.* Thousand Oaks, Calif.: Sage.

Robins, S. 2002. "A Consultant's Guide to Understanding and Promoting Emotional Intelligence in the Workplace." In R. Lowman, ed., *Handbook of Organizational Consulting Psychology.* San Francisco: Jossey-Bass.

Rosenzweig, P. 2004. "What Do We Think Happened at ABB? Pitfalls in Research about Firm Performance." *International Journal of Management and Decision Making* 5 (4): 267–281.

———. 2007. *The Halo Effect.* New York, N.Y.: Free Press.

Sartain, L. 2003. *HR from the Heart.* New York: American Management Association.

Schaffer, R. 2002. *High-Impact Consulting,* San Francisco: Jossey-Bass.

Schaffer, R., and R. Ashkenas. 2005. *Rapid Results.* San Francisco: Jossey-Bass.

Scheier, M., and C. Carver. 1985. "Optimism, Coping, and Health: Assessment and Implications of Generalized Outcome Expectancies." *Health Psychology* 4: 219–247.

Schein, E. 1969. *Process Consultation: Its Role in Organization Development.* Reading, Mass.: Addison-Wesley.

———. 1985. *Organizational Culture and Leadership.* San Francisco: Jossey-Bass.

———. 1988. *Process Consultation,* Volume I: *Its Role in Organization Development.* Reading, Mass.: Addison-Wesley.

———. 1999. *Process Consultation Revisited: Building the Helping Relationship.* Reading, Mass.: Addison-Wesley-Longman.

———. 2004. *Organizational Culture and Leaders.* San Francisco: Jossey-Bass.

———. 2005. "Organizational Development: A Wedding of Anthropology and Organizational Therapy." In D. Bradford and W. Burke, eds., *Reinventing Organization Development: New Approaches to Change in Organizations/Addressing the Crisis, Achieving the Potential,* pp. 131–143. San Francisco: Pfeiffer.

Scott, C., and J. Hawk, eds. 1986. *Heal Thyself: The Health of Health Care Professionals.* New York: Brunner Mazel.

Segerstrom, S., S. Taylor, M. Kemeny, and J. Fahey. 1998. "Optimism Is Associated with Mood, Coping, and Immune Change in Response to Stress." *Journal of Personality and Social Psychology* 74: 1646–1655.

Seligman, M. 1998. *Learned Optimism.* New York: Pocket Books.

Seward, B. 2000. *Managing Stress in Emergency Medical Services.* Sudbury, Mass.: American Academy of Orthopedic Surgeons.

Snyder, C., C. Harris, J. Anderson, S. Holleran, L. Irving, and S. Sigmon. 1991. "The Will and the Ways: Development and Validation of an Individual Differences Measure of Hope." *Journal of Personality and Social Psychology* 60: 570–585.

Sotile, W., and M. Sotile. 2002. *The Resilient Physician: Emotional Management for Doctors and Their Medical Organizations.* Chicago: American Medical Association.

Spector, P., and S. Fox. 2005. *Counterproductive Work Behavior: Investigations of Actors and Targets.* Washington, D.C.: American Psychological Association.

Sturdy, A. 1997. "The Consultancy Process—An Insecure Business." *Journal of Management Studies* 34 (3): 389–413.

Sutton, R. 2007. *The No Asshole Rule: Building a Civilized Workplace and Surviving One That Isn't.* New York: Warner Business Books.

Tedeschi, R., C. Park, and L. Calhoun. 1998. *Posttraumatic Growth: Positive Changes in the Aftermath of Crisis.* Mahwah, N.J.: Lawrence Erlbaum.

Tooby, J., and L. Cosmides. 1990. "The Past Explains the Present: Emotional Adaptations and the Structure of Ancestral Environments." *Ethology and Sociobiology* 11: 375–424.

Van Fleet, D., and R. Griffin. 2006. "Dysfunctional Organization Culture: The Role of Leadership in Motivating Dysfunctional Work Behaviors." *Journal of Managerial Psychology* 21 (8): 698–708.

Van Fleet, D., and E. Van Fleet. 2007. "Internal Terrorists: The Terrorists Inside Organizations." *Journal of Managerial Psychology* 21 (8): 763–774.

Vardi, Y., and E. Weitz. 2004. *Misbehavior in Organizations: Theory, Research and Management.* Mahwah, N.J.: Lawrence Erlbaum.

Vardi, Y., and Y. Wiener. 1996. "Misbehavior in Organizations: A Motivational Framework." *Organization Science* 7: 151–165.

Von Bertalanffy, L. 1950. "The Theory of Open Systems in Physics and Biology." *Science* 13: 23–29.

Watzlawick, P., J. Beavin, and D. Jackson. 1967. *Pragmatics of Human Communication.* New York: W. W. Norton.

Whetten, D., and K. Cameron. 2007. *Developing Management Skills.* Englewood Cliffs, N.J.: Pearson/Prentice Hall.

Whicker, M. 1996. *Toxic Leaders: When Organizations Go Bad.* Westport, Conn.: Quorum Books.

Whitney, D., A. Trosten-Bloom, and D. Cooperrider. 2003. *The Power of Appreciative Inquiry.* San Francisco: Berrett-Koehler.

Wicks, R. 2002. *Riding the Dragon.* Notre Dame, Ind.: Sorin Books.

———. 2006. *Overcoming Secondary Stress in Medical and Nursing Practice: A Guide to Professional Resilience and Personal Well-Being.* New York: Oxford University Press.

Wilder, C., and S. Collins. 1994. "Patterns of Interactional Paradoxes." In W. Cupach and B. Spitzberg, eds., *The Dark Side of Interpersonal Communication.* Hillsdale, N.J.: Lawrence Erlbaum.

Wishbow, N. 1987. "Applying the Concept of the Double Bind to Communication Organizations." In S. Thomas, ed., *Studies in Communication,* Volume 3, pp. 114–157. Norwood, N.J.: Ablex.

Wood, J., A. Mathews, and T. Dalgleish. 2001. "Anxiety and Cognitive Inhibition." *Emotion* 1 (2): 166–181.

Zaleznik, A. 2007. "The Case for Not Interpreting Unconscious Mental Life in Consulting to Organizations." In M. Kets de Vries, K. Korotov, and E. Florent-Treacy, eds., *Coach and Couch*, pp. 320–342. Houndmills, Basingstoke, Hampshire, U.K.: Palgrave Macmillan.

Zerbe, W., C. Hartel, and N. Ashkanasy, eds. 2008. *Research on Emotion in Organizations*, Volume 4: *Emotions, Ethics and Decision-Making.* Bingley, U.K.: Emerald.

Index